DOVER · THRIFT · EDITIONS

100 Best~Loved Poems

Edited by Philip Smith

Happy Holidays from your friends at Target
Many thanks for participating in our
Holiday Happening 1999

DOVER PUBLICATIONS, INC.
Mineola, New York

DOVER THRIFT EDITIONS

GENERAL EDITOR: STANLEY APPELBAUM
EDITOR OF THIS VOLUME: PHILIP SMITH

ACKNOWLEDGMENTS: see page iv.

Copyright

Published in Canada by General Publishing Company, Ltd., 30 Lesmill Road, Don Mills, Toronto, Ontario.

Published in the United Kingdom by Constable and Company, Ltd., 3 The Lanchesters, 162–164 Fulham Palace Road, London W6 9ER.

Bibliographical Note

100 Best-Loved Poems is a new anthology, first published by Dover Publications, Inc., in 1995.

Library of Congress Cataloging-in-Publication Data

100 best-loved poems / edited by Philip Smith.
    p.   cm. — (Dover thrift editions)
  Includes index.
  ISBN 0-486-28553-7 (pbk.)
  1. English poetry.   2. American poetry.   I. Smith, Philip, 1967–   II. Series.
PR1175.A137   1995
821.008 — dc20   95–19647
                                                                        CIP

Manufactured in the United States of America
Dover Publications, Inc., 31 East 2nd Street, Mineola, N.Y. 11501

Note

This volume contains a chronological selection of one hundred of the greatest and best-loved poems in the English language. These works provide a concise overview of the development of verse writing in the British Isles and America from the Renaissance until the early twentieth century, and include many lines and phrases that have become proverbial in everyday speech. Although no single volume can possibly provide a thorough introduction to such a vast and complex subject, it may be argued that familiarity with a majority of the poems in this collection is to be expected of any English-speaking person professing a literary education.

In making a selection as concise as the present, far more poems and poets must be omitted than included. Longer poems (such as John Milton's *Paradise Lost*), which contain some of the finest writing in the language, are excluded for want of space. Readers who enjoy the poems herein are encouraged to explore the lofty heights of thought and expression manifested in extended poetic works, as well as the vast ranges of experience recorded in the countless other poems not included in this volume.

It is also acknowledged that this anthology reflects a specific cultural tradition in British and American writing, and makes no effort to represent the cultural plurality that is increasingly recognized in the literatures of those nations. It is hoped that readers of all backgrounds will gain more from the resulting aesthetic continuity displayed than would be possible from a selection broader but more diffuse in scope.

Acknowledgments

Contents

100 BEST-LOVED POEMS

BALLADS

Ballads are anonymous, frequently tragic, storytelling songs that often developed for centuries before being recorded in writing. The following are two of the most famous English ballads, dating probably from the late Middle Ages.

Lord Randal

"O where hae ye been, Lord Randal, my son?
O where hae ye been, my handsome young man?"
"I hae been to the wild wood; mother, make my bed soon,
For I'm weary wi' hunting, and fain wald lie down."

"Where gat ye your dinner, Lord Randal, my son?
Where gat ye your dinner, my handsome young man?"
"I din'd wi' my true-love; mother, make my bed soon,
For I'm weary wi' hunting, and fain wald lie down."

"What gat ye to your dinner, Lord Randal, my son?
What gat ye to your dinner, my handsome young man?"
"I gat eels boil'd in broo;[1] mother, make my bed soon,
For I'm weary wi' hunting, and fain wald lie down."

"What became of your bloodhounds, Lord Randal, my son?
What became of your bloodhounds, my handsome young man?"
"O they swell'd and they died; mother, make my bed soon,
For I'm weary wi' hunting, and fain wald lie down."

"O I fear ye are poison'd, Lord Randal, my son!
I fear ye are poison'd, my handsome young man!"
"O yes! I am poison'd; mother, make my bed soon,
For I'm sick at the heart, and I fain wald lie down."

---

[1] *broo*] broth.

Sir Patrick Spens

I. THE SAILING

The king sits in Dunfermline town
  Drinking the blude-red[1] wine;
"O whare will I get a skeely[2] skipper
  To sail this new ship o' mine?"

O up and spak an eldern knight,
  Sat at the king's right knee;
"Sir Patrick Spens is the best sailor
  That ever sail'd the sea."

Our king has written a braid[3] letter,
  And seal'd it with his hand,
And sent it to Sir Patrick Spens,
  Was walking on the strand.

"To Noroway, to Noroway,
  To Noroway o'er the faem;[4]
The king's daughter o' Noroway,
  'Tis thou must bring her hame."

The first word that Sir Patrick read
  So loud, loud laugh'd he;
The neist[5] word that Sir Patrick read
  The tear blinded his e'e.

"O wha is this has done this deed
  And tauld the king o' me,
To send us out, at this time o' year,
  To sail upon the sea?

"Be it wind, be it weet,[6] be it hail, be it sleet,
  Our ship must sail the faem;
The king's daughter o' Noroway,
  'Tis we must fetch her hame."

---

[1] *blude-red*] blood-red.
[2] *skeely*] skillful.
[3] *braid*] broad.
[4] *faem*] foam.
[5] *neist*] next.
[6] *weet*] wet.

They hoysed[7] their sails on Monenday morn
   Wi' a' the speed they may;
They hae landed in Noroway
   Upon a Wodensday.

II. THE RETURN

"Mak ready, mak ready, my merry men a'!
   Our gude[8] ship sails the morn."
"Now ever alack, my master dear,
   I fear a deadly storm.

"I saw the new moon late yestreen[9]
   Wi' the auld moon in her arm;
And if we gang to sea, master,
   I fear we'll come to harm."

They hadna sail'd a league, a league,
   A league but barely three,
When the lift[10] grew dark, and the wind blew loud,
   And gurly[11] grew the sea.

The ankers brak, and the topmast lap,[12]
   It was sic a deadly storm:
And the waves cam owre the broken ship
   Till a' her sides were torn.

"Go fetch a web o' the silken claith,
   Another o' the twine,
And wap them into our ship's side,
   And let nae the sea come in."

They fetch'd a web o' the silken claith,
   Another o' the twine,
And they wapp'd them round that gude ship's side,
   But still the sea came in.

---

[7] *hoysed*] hoisted.
[8] *gude*] good.
[9] *yestreen*] yesterday evening.
[10] *lift*] sky.
[11] *gurly*] grim, surly.
[12] *lap*] leaped.

O laith,[13] laith were our gude Scots lords
   To wet their cork-heel'd shoon;[14]
But lang or a' the play was play'd
   They wat their hats aboon.[15]

And mony was the feather bed
   That flatter'd[16] on the faem;
And mony was the gude lord's son
   That never mair cam hame.

O lang, lang may the ladies sit,
   Wi' their fans into their hand,
Before they see Sir Patrick Spens
   Come sailing to the strand!

And lang, lang may the maidens sit
   Wi' their gowd kames[17] in their hair,
A-waiting for their ain dear loves!
   For them they'll see nae mair.

Half-owre,[18] half-owre to Aberdour,
   'Tis fifty fathoms deep;
And there lies gude Sir Patrick Spens,
   Wi' the Scots lords at his feet!

SIR THOMAS WYATT *(1503–1542)*

A courtier and diplomat active in the court of King Henry VIII, Wyatt is credited
with introducing Italian sonnet forms to English literature in the 1530s.

The Lover Showeth How He Is Forsaken of Such as He Sometime Enjoyed

They flee from me that sometime did me seek,
   With naked foot stalking in my chamber.
I have seen them gentle, tame, and meek,

---

[13] *laith*] loath.
[14] *shoon*] shoes.
[15] *aboon*] above.
[16] *flatter'd*] floated.
[17] *gowd kames*] gold combs.
[18] *half-owre*] halfway.

That now are wild, and do not once remember
That sometime they have put themselves in danger
To take bread at my hand; and now they range,
Busily seeking with a continual change.

Thank'd be fortune, it hath been otherwise
    Twenty times better; but once, in special,
In thin array, after a pleasant guise,
    When her loose gown from her shoulders did fall,
    And she me caught in her arms long and small,
Therewith all sweetly did me kiss,
And softly said, 'Dear heart, how like you this?'

It was no dream; I lay broad waking:
    But all is turn'd, thorough my gentleness,
Into a strange fashion of forsaking;
    And I have leave to go, of her goodness;
    And she also to use new-fangleness.
But since that I so unkindly am served,
I fain would know what *she* hath deserved.

CHRISTOPHER MARLOWE *(1564–1593)*

Second only to Shakespeare (whom he inspired) as an Elizabethan dramatist, Marlowe penned some of the earliest and greatest English-language tragedies before being killed in a tavern at age 29.

The Passionate Shepherd to His Love

Come live with me and be my Love,
And we will all the pleasures prove
That hills and valleys, dales and fields,
Or woods or steepy mountain yields.

And we will sit upon the rocks,
And see the shepherds feed their flocks
By shallow rivers, to whose falls
Melodious birds sing madrigals.

And I will make thee beds of roses
And a thousand fragrant posies;
A cap of flowers, and a kirtle
Embroider'd all with leaves of myrtle.

A gown made of the finest wool
Which from our pretty lambs we pull;
Fair-lined slippers for the cold,
With buckles of the purest gold.

A belt of straw and ivy-buds
With coral clasps and amber studs:
And if these pleasures may thee move,
Come live with me and be my Love.

The shepherd swains shall dance and sing
For thy delight each May morning:
If these delights thy mind may move,
Then live with me and be my Love.

WILLIAM SHAKESPEARE *(1564–1616)*

The preeminent English poet and playwright, Shakespeare published a sequence of
154 sonnets in 1609 that continue to be regarded as the highest perfection of the
form in English.

Sonnet XVIII

Shall I compare thee to a summer's day?
Thou art more lovely and more temperate:
Rough winds do shake the darling buds of May,
And summer's lease hath all too short a date:
Sometime too hot the eye of heaven shines,
And often is his gold complexion dimm'd;
And every fair from fair sometime declines,
By chance or nature's changing course untrimm'd;
But thy eternal summer shall not fade,
Nor lose possession of that fair thou owest;
Nor shall Death brag thou wander'st in his shade,
When in eternal lines to time thou grow'st:
    So long as men can breathe, or eyes can see,
    So long lives this, and this gives life to thee.

Sonnet LXXIII

That time of year thou mayst in me behold
When yellow leaves, or none, or few, do hang
Upon those boughs which shake against the cold,
Bare ruin'd choirs, where late the sweet birds sang.
In me thou see'st the twilight of such day
As after sunset fadeth in the west;
Which by and by black night doth take away,
Death's second self, that seals up all in rest.
In me thou see'st the glowing of such fire,
That on the ashes of his youth doth lie,
As the death-bed whereon it must expire,
Consumed with that which it was nourish'd by.
   This thou perceivest, which makes thy love more strong,
   To love that well which thou must leave ere long.

Sonnet XCIV

They that have power to hurt and will do none,
That do not do the thing they most do show,
Who, moving others, are themselves as stone,
Unmoved, cold and to temptation slow;
They rightly do inherit heaven's graces
And husband nature's riches from expense;
They are the lords and owners of their faces,
Others but stewards of their excellence.
The summer's flower is to the summer sweet,
Though to itself it only live and die,
But if that flower with base infection meet,
The basest weed outbraves his dignity:
   For sweetest things turn sourest by their deeds;
   Lilies that fester smell far worse than weeds.

Sonnet CXVI

Let me not to the marriage of true minds
Admit impediments. Love is not love
Which alters when it alteration finds,
Or bends with the remover to remove:
O, no! it is an ever-fixed mark,

That looks on tempests and is never shaken;
It is the star to every wandering bark,
Whose worth's unknown, although his height be taken.
Love's not Time's fool, though rosy lips and cheeks
Within his bending sickle's compass come;
Love alters not with his brief hours and weeks,
But bears it out even to the edge of doom.
    If this be error and upon me proved,
      I never writ, nor no man ever loved.

THOMAS NASHE *(1567–1601)*

During a tempestuous and brief career, Nashe produced plays, satire, pamphlets and a novel as well as poetry. The following lyric is taken from his comedy *Summer's Last Will and Testament* (1592).

"Adieu, Farewell Earth's Bliss"

Adieu, farewell earth's bliss;
This world uncertain is;
Fond are life's lustful joys;
Death proves them all but toys;
None from his darts can fly;
I am sick, I must die.
    Lord, have mercy on us!

Rich men, trust not in wealth,
Gold cannot buy you health;
Physic himself must fade.
All things to end are made,
The plague full swift goes by;
I am sick, I must die.
    Lord, have mercy on us!

Beauty is but a flower
Which wrinkles will devour;
Brightness falls from the air;
Queens have died young and fair;
Dust hath closed Helen's eye.
I am sick, I must die.
    Lord, have mercy on us!

Strength stoops unto the grave,
Worms feed on Hector brave;
Swords may not fight with fate,
Earth still holds ope her gate.
"Come, come" the bells do cry.
I am sick, I must die.
    Lord, have mercy on us.

Wit with his wantonness
Tasteth death's bitterness;
Hell's executioner
Hath no ears for to hear
What vain art can reply.
I am sick, I must die.
    Lord, have mercy on us.

Haste, therefore, each degree,
To welcome destiny;
Heaven is our heritage,
Earth but a player's stage;
Mount we unto the sky.
I am sick, I must die.
    Lord, have mercy on us.

JOHN DONNE (1572–1631)

Born a Catholic, Donne became an Anglican cleric of great influence. He also wrote secular as well as religious poetry that combined brilliant craftsmanship, heartfelt emotion and intellectual rigor while addressing issues of love and faith.

The Good Morrow

I wonder by my troth, what thou, and I
Did, till we lov'd? were we not wean'd till then?
But suck'd on country pleasures, childishly?
Or snorted we in the seven sleepers' den?
'Twas so; but this, all pleasures fancies be.
If ever any beauty I did see,
Which I desir'd, and got, 'twas but a dream of thee.

And now good morrow to our waking souls,
Which watch not one another out of fear;
For love, all love of other sights controls,
And makes one little room, an everywhere.
Let sea-discoverers to new worlds have gone,
Let maps to other, worlds on worlds have shown,
Let us possess one world, each hath one, and is one.

My face in thine eye, thine in mine appears,
And true plain hearts do in the faces rest,
Where can we find two better hemispheres
Without sharp north, without declining west?
Whatever dies, was not mix'd equally;
If our two loves be one, or, thou and I
Love so alike, that none do slacken, none can die.

Holy Sonnet X

Death be not proud, though some have called thee
Mighty and dreadful, for, thou art not so,
For, those, whom thou think'st, thou dost overthrow,
Die not, poor death, nor yet canst thou kill me.
From rest and sleep, which but thy pictures be,
Much pleasure, then from thee, much more must flow,
And soonest our best men with thee do go,
Rest of their bones, and soul's delivery.
Thou art slave to fate, chance, kings, and desperate men,
And dost with poison, war, and sickness dwell,
And poppy, or charms can make us sleep as well,
And better than thy stroke; why swell'st thou then?
One short sleep past, we wake eternally,
And death shall be no more; death, thou shalt die.

Holy Sonnet XIV

Batter my heart, three-person'd God; for, you
As yet but knock, breathe, shine, and seek to mend;
That I may rise, and stand, o'erthrow me, and bend
Your force, to break, blow, burn and make me new.
I, like an usurp'd town, t'another due,
Labour to admit you, but oh, to no end,

Reason your viceroy in me, me should defend,
But is captiv'd, and proves weak or untrue.
Yet dearly I love you, and would be loved fain,
But am betroth'd unto your enemy:
Divorce me, untie, or break that knot again,
Take me to you, imprison me, for I
Except you enthrall me, never shall be free,
Nor ever chaste, except you ravish me.

BEN JONSON *(1572–1637)*

At his peak the leading literary figure of his day, Jonson was an associate of Shakespeare, Donne and other distinguished persons, as well as poet laureate. He was an accomplished playwright, translator and critic, and also wrote great lyric poetry.

To Celia

Drink to me, only, with thine eyes,
    And I will pledge with mine;
Or leave a kiss but in the cup
    And I'll not look for wine.
The thirst that from the soul doth rise
    Doth ask a drink divine;
But might I of Jove's nectar sup,
    I would not change for thine.

I sent thee late a rosy wreath,
    Not so much honouring thee
As giving it a hope that there
    It could not wither'd be;
But thou thereon didst only breathe,
    And sent'st it back to me;
Since when it grows, and smells, I swear,
    Not of itself but thee!

On My First Son

Farewell, thou child of my right hand, and joy;
    My sin was too much hope of thee, lov'd boy.
Seven years thou wert lent to me, and I thee pay,
    Exacted by thy fate, on the just day.
Oh, could I lose all father now! For why
    Will man lament the state he should envy?
To have so soon 'scaped world's and flesh's rage,
    And, if no other misery, yet age?
Rest in soft peace, and, asked, say here doth lie
    Ben Jonson his best piece of poetry;
For whose sake, henceforth, all his vows be such,
    As what he loves may never like too much.

ROBERT HERRICK *(1591–1674)*

One of Ben Jonson's many followers, Herrick did not let his position as an Anglican cleric deter his composing sensual lyrics (of which the following is a mild example) that celebrate the earthly pleasures of human existence.

To the Virgins, to Make Much of Time

Gather ye rosebuds while ye may,
    Old Time is still a-flying:
And this same flower that smiles to-day
    To-morrow will be dying.

The glorious lamp of heaven, the sun,
    The higher he's a-getting,
The sooner will his race be run,
    And nearer he's to setting.

That age is best which is the first,
    When youth and blood are warmer;
But being spent, the worse, and worst
    Times still succeed the former.

Then be not coy, but use your time,
    And while ye may, go marry:
For having lost but once your prime,
    You may for ever tarry.

Upon Julia's Clothes

Whenas in silks my Julia goes,
Then, then, methinks, how sweetly flows
The liquefaction of her clothes!

Next, when I cast mine eyes and see
That brave vibration each way free,
— O how that glittering taketh me!

GEORGE HERBERT (1593–1633)

Like his contemporary Herrick, an Anglican clergyman as well as poet, Herbert
stood in contrast to the former as a model of virtue, piety and devotion. This poem
uses secular imagery to probe a religious question.

Love Bade Me Welcome

Love bade me welcome; yet my soul drew back,
    Guilty of dust and sin.
But quick-eyed Love, observing me grow slack
    From my first entrance in,
Drew nearer to me, sweetly questioning
    If I lacked any thing.

"A guest," I answered, "worthy to be here";
    Love said, "You shall be he."
"I the unkind, ungrateful? Ah my dear,
    I cannot look on Thee."
Love took my hand, and smiling did reply,
    "Who made the eyes but I?"

"Truth Lord, but I have marred them: let my shame
    Go where it doth deserve."
"And know you not," says Love, "who bore the blame?"
    "My dear, then I will serve."
"You must sit down," says Love, "and taste My meat."
    So I did sit and eat.

EDMUND WALLER *(1606–1687)*

Waller was a Royalist lawyer and politician whose poetry was first published in 1645, while he was in political exile. He is credited with bringing a new level of technical mastery to English verse.

Song

Go, lovely Rose—
Tell her that wastes her time and me,
    That now she knows,
When I resemble her to thee,
How sweet and fair she seems to be.

Tell her that's young,
And shuns to have her graces spied,
    That hadst thou sprung
In deserts where no men abide,
Thou must have uncommended died.

Small is the worth
Of beauty from the light retired:
    Bid her come forth,
Suffer herself to be desired,
And not blush so to be admired.

Then die—that she
The common fate of all things rare
    May read in thee;
How small a part of time they share
That are so wondrous sweet and fair!

JOHN MILTON *(1608–1674)*

Best known as the Puritan author of the epic poem *Paradise Lost*, Milton excelled in short forms as well. His relatively few sonnets include some of the finest in the language.

On His Blindness

When I consider how my light is spent
    Ere half my days in this dark world and wide,
    And that one Talent which is death to hide
    Lodged with me useless, though my soul more bent
To serve therewith my Maker, and present

My true account, lest He returning chide,
    "Doth God exact day-labour, light denied?"
I fondly ask. But Patience, to prevent
That murmur, soon replies, "God doth not need
    Either man's work or his own gifts. Who best
    Bear his mild yoke, they serve him best. His state
Is kingly: thousands at his bidding speed,
    And post o'er land and ocean without rest;
    They also serve who only stand and wait."

On His Deceased Wife

Methought I saw my late espousèd saint
    Brought to me like Alcestis from the grave,
    Whom Jove's great son to her glad husband gave,
    Rescued from Death by force, though pale and faint.[1]
Mine, as whom washed from spot of childbed taint
    Purification in the Old Law did save,
    And such as yet once more I trust to have
    Full sight of her in Heaven without restraint,
Came vested all in white, pure as her mind.
    Her face was veiled; yet to my fancied sight
    Love, sweetness, goodness, in her person shined
So clear as in no face with more delight.
    But, oh! as to embrace me she inclined,
    I waked, she fled, and day brought back my night.

SIR JOHN SUCKLING *(1609–1642)*

Grouped with Richard Lovelace as a leading "Cavalier" poet (his political involvements forced him to flee the country), Suckling wrote plays and poetry that are notable for their refinement and polished ease.

"Why So Pale and Wan, Fond Lover?"

Why so pale and wan, fond lover?
      Prithee, why so pale?
Will, when looking well can't move her,
      Looking ill prevail?
      Prithee, why so pale?

---

[1] Herakles (Hercules) brought Alcestis back from the dead to her husband Admetus.

Why so dull and mute, young sinner?
    Prithee, why so mute?
Will, when speaking well can't win her,
    Saying nothing do 't?
    Prithee, why so mute?

Quit, quit for shame! This will not move;
    This cannot take her.
If of herself she will not love,
    Nothing can make her:
    The devil take her!

RICHARD LOVELACE *(1618–1658)*

Like Suckling, an active Royalist, Lovelace wrote poems based on his unhappy experiences, including warfare and imprisonment, that combine sentiments of courtly love with political gallantry.

To Lucasta, Going to the Wars

Tell me not, Sweet, I am unkind,
    That from the nunnery
Of thy chaste breast and quiet mind
    To war and arms I fly.

True, a new mistress now I chase,
    The first foe in the field;
And with a stronger faith embrace
    A sword, a horse, a shield.

Yet this inconstancy is such
    As thou too shalt adore;
I could not love thee, Dear, so much,
    Loved I not Honour more.

ANDREW MARVELL *(1621–1678)*

Better known as a politician than a poet until the twentieth century, Marvell was a Member of Parliament whose greatest works were not published until after his death. "To His Coy Mistress" playfully combines sensuality with more serious themes.

To His Coy Mistress

Had we but world enough, and time,
This coyness, Lady, were no crime.
We would sit down and think which way
To walk and pass our long love's day.
Thou by the Indian Ganges' side
Shouldst rubies find: I by the tide
Of Humber would complain. I would
Love you ten years before the Flood,
And you should, if you please, refuse
Till the conversion of the Jews.
My vegetable love should grow
Vaster than empires, and more slow;
An hundred years should go to praise
Thine eyes and on thy forehead gaze;
Two hundred to adore each breast;
But thirty thousand to the rest;
An age at least to every part,
And the last age should show your heart;
For, Lady, you deserve this state,
Nor would I love at lower rate.
    But at my back I always hear
Time's winged chariot hurrying near;
And yonder all before us lie
Deserts of vast eternity.
Thy beauty shall no more be found,
Nor, in thy marble vault, shall sound
My echoing song: then worms shall try
That long preserved virginity,
And your quaint honour turn to dust,
And into ashes all my lust:
The grave's a fine and private place,
But none, I think, do there embrace.
    Now therefore, while the youthful hue
Sits on thy skin like morning dew,

And while thy willing soul transpires
At every pore with instant fires,
Now let us sport us while we may,
And now, like amorous birds of prey,
Rather at once our time devour
Than languish in his slow-chapt[1] power.
Let us roll all our strength and all
Our sweetness up into one ball,
And tear our pleasures with rough strife
Thorough the iron gates of life:
Thus, though we cannot make our sun
Stand still, yet we will make him run.

HENRY VAUGHAN *(1621–1695)*

Vaughan was a Welsh physician of hermetic leanings whose verses contain occult and alchemical themes. Greatly influenced by the more pious George Herbert, Vaughan was in turn a shaping force upon Wordsworth.

The Retreat

Happy those early days! when I
Shined in my angel-infancy.
Before I understood this place
Appointed for my second race,
Or taught my soul to fancy ought
But a white, celestial thought,
When yet I had not walked above
A mile or two, from my first love,
And looking back (at that short space)
Could see a glimpse of his bright face;
When on some *gilded cloud* or *flower*
My gazing soul would dwell an hour,
And in those weaker glories spy
Some shadows of eternity;
Before I taught my tongue to wound
My conscience with a sinful sound,
Or had the black art to dispense
A sev'ral sin to ev'ry sense,

---

[1] *slow-chapt*] slowly devouring.

But felt through all this fleshly dress
Bright *shoots* of everlastingness.
  O, how I long to travel back
And tread again that ancient track!
That I might once more reach that plain,
Where first I left my glorious train;
From whence th' inlightened spirit sees
That shady city of palm trees;
But (ah!) my soul with too much stay
Is drunk, and staggers in the way.
Some men a forward motion love,
But I by backward steps would move,
And when this dust falls to the urn
In that state I came, return.

THOMAS GRAY *(1716–1771)*

An important precursor of the Romantics, this retiring poet achieved instant celebrity with the publication in 1751 of his "Elegy Written in a Country Churchyard," which remains one of English literature's most famous and imitated works.

Elegy Written in a Country Churchyard

The Curfew tolls the knell of parting day,
  The lowing herd wind slowly o'er the lea,
The plowman homeward plods his weary way,
  And leaves the world to darkness and to me.

Now fades the glimmering landscape on the sight,
  And all the air a solemn stillness holds,
Save where the beetle wheels his droning flight,
  And drowsy tinklings lull the distant folds;

Save that from yonder ivy-mantled tow'r
  The moping owl does to the moon complain
Of such as, wand'ring near her secret bow'r,
  Molest her ancient solitary reign.

Beneath those rugged elms, that yew-tree's shade,
  Where heaves the turf in many a mould'ring heap,
Each in his narrow cell for ever laid,
  The rude Forefathers of the hamlet sleep.

The breezy call of incense-breathing Morn,
  The swallow twitt'ring from the straw-built shed,
The cock's shrill clarion, or the echoing horn,
  No more shall rouse them from their lowly bed.

For them no more the blazing hearth shall burn,
  Or busy housewife ply her evening care:
No children run to lisp their sire's return,
  Or climb his knees the envied kiss to share.

Oft did the harvest to their sickle yield,
  Their furrow oft the stubborn glebe has broke:
How jocund did they drive their team afield!
  How bow'd the woods beneath their sturdy stroke!

Let not Ambition mock their useful toil,
  Their homely joys, and destiny obscure;
Nor Grandeur hear with a disdainful smile
  The short and simple annals of the poor.

The boast of heraldry, the pomp of pow'r,
  And all that beauty, all that wealth e'er gave,
Awaits alike th' inevitable hour:
  The paths of glory lead but to the grave.

Nor you, ye Proud, impute to These the fault,
  If Memory o'er their Tomb no Trophies raise,
Where through the long-drawn aisle and fretted vault
  The pealing anthem swells the note of praise.

Can storied urn or animated bust
  Back to its mansion call the fleeting breath?
Can Honour's voice provoke the silent dust,
  Or Flatt'ry soothe the dull cold ear of death?

Perhaps in this neglected spot is laid
  Some heart once pregnant with celestial fire;
Hands, that the rod of empire might have sway'd,
  Or waked to ecstasy the living lyre.

But Knowledge to their eyes her ample page
  Rich with the spoils of time did ne'er unroll;
Chill Penury repress'd their noble rage,
  And froze the genial current of the soul.

Full many a gem of purest ray serene
  The dark unfathom'd caves of ocean bear:

Full many a flower is born to blush unseen,
   And waste its sweetness on the desert air.

Some village Hampden that with dauntless breast
   The little tyrant of his fields withstood,
Some mute inglorious Milton, here may rest,
   Some Cromwell guiltless of his country's blood.

Th' applause of list'ning senates to command,
   The threats of pain and ruin to despise,
To scatter plenty o'er a smiling land,
   And read their history in a nation's eyes,

Their lot forbade: nor circumscribed alone
   Their growing virtues, but their crimes confined;
Forbade to wade through slaughter to a throne,
   And shut the gates of mercy on mankind,

The struggling pangs of conscious truth to hide,
   To quench the blushes of ingenuous shame,
Or heap the shrine of Luxury and Pride
   With incense kindled at the Muse's flame.

Far from the madding crowd's ignoble strife
   Their sober wishes never learn'd to stray;
Along the cool sequester'd vale of life
   They kept the noiseless tenor of their way.

Yet ev'n these bones from insult to protect
   Some frail memorial still erected nigh,
With uncouth rhymes and shapeless sculpture deck'd,
   Implores the passing tribute of a sigh.

Their name, their years, spelt by th' unletter'd muse,
   The place of fame and elegy supply:
And many a holy text around she strews,
   That teach the rustic moralist to die.

For who, to dumb Forgetfulness a prey,
   This pleasing anxious being e'er resign'd,
Left the warm precincts of the cheerful day,
   Nor cast one longing ling'ring look behind?

On some fond breast the parting soul relies,
   Some pious drops the closing eye requires;
E'en from the tomb the voice of Nature cries,
   E'en in our Ashes live their wonted Fires.

For thee, who, mindful of th' unhonour'd dead,
    Dost in these lines their artless tale relate;
If chance, by lonely contemplation led,
    Some kindred spirit shall inquire thy fate,

Haply some hoary-headed Swain may say,
    "Oft have we seen him at the peep of dawn
Brushing with hasty steps the dews away
    To meet the sun upon the upland lawn.

"There at the foot of yonder nodding beech
    That wreathes its old fantastic roots so high,
His listless length at noontide would he stretch,
    And pore upon the brook that babbles by.

"Hard by yon wood, now smiling as in scorn,
    Mutt'ring his wayward fancies he would rove,
Now drooping, woeful wan, like one forlorn,
    Or crazed with care, or cross'd in hopeless love.

"One morn I miss'd him on the custom'd hill,
    Along the heath and near his fav'rite tree;
Another came; nor yet beside the rill,
    Nor up the lawn, nor at the wood was he;

"The next with dirges due in sad array
    Slow through the church-way path we saw him borne.
Approach and read (for thou canst read) the lay
    Graved on the stone beneath yon aged thorn."

THE EPITAPH

Here rests his head upon the lap of Earth
    A Youth to Fortune and to Fame unknown.
Fair Science frown'd not on his humble birth,
    And Melancholy mark'd him for her own.

Large was his bounty, and his soul sincere,
    Heav'n did a recompense as largely send:
He gave to Mis'ry all he had, a tear,
    He gain'd from Heav'n ('twas all he wish'd) a friend.

No farther seek his merits to disclose,
    Or draw his frailties from their dread abode
(There they alike in trembling hope repose),
    The bosom of his Father and his God.

Ode on the Death of a Favourite Cat, Drowned in a Tub of Gold Fishes

'Twas on a lofty vase's side,
Where China's gayest art had dyed
  The azure flowers that blow;
Demurest of the tabby kind,
The pensive Selima reclined,
  Gazed on the lake below.

Her conscious tail her joy declared;
The fair round face, the snowy beard,
  The velvet of her paws,
Her coat, that with the tortoise vies,
Her ears of jet, and emerald eyes,
  She saw; and purr'd applause.

Still had she gazed; but 'midst the tide
Two angel forms were seen to glide,
  The Genii of the stream:
Their scaly armor's Tyrian hue
Thro' richest purple to the view
  Betray'd a golden gleam.

The hapless Nymph with wonder saw:
A whisker first and then a claw,
  With many an ardent wish,
She stretch'd in vain to reach the prize.
What female heart can gold despise?
  What Cat's averse to fish?

Presumptuous Maid! with looks intent
Again she stretch'd, again she bent,
  Nor knew the gulf between.
(Malignant Fate sat by, and smil'd)
The slipp'ry verge her feet beguil'd,
  She tumbled headlong in.

Eight times emerging from the flood
She mew'd to ev'ry wat'ry God,
  Some speedy aid to send.
No Dolphin came, no Nereid stirr'd:
Nor cruel *Tom*, nor *Susan* heard.
  A Fav'rite has no friend!

From hence, ye Beauties, undeceiv'd,
Know, one false step is ne'er retriev'd,
   And be with caution bold.
Not all that tempts your wand'ring eyes
And heedless hearts, is lawful prize;
   Nor all, that glisters, gold.

WILLIAM BLAKE (1757–1827)

An important visionary artist who published vividly illustrated editions of his writings, and one of the most original of English poets, Blake was dismissed as a madman in his day. In addition to short poems of unmatched inspiration he wrote lengthy and difficult verse prophecies.

The Lamb

   Little Lamb, who made thee?
   Dost thou know who made thee?
Gave thee life & bid thee feed,
By the stream & o'er the mead;
Gave thee clothing of delight,
Softest clothing, wooly, bright;
Gave thee such a tender voice,
Making all the vales rejoice?
   Little Lamb, who made thee?
   Dost thou know who made thee?

   Little Lamb, I'll tell thee,
   Little Lamb, I'll tell thee:
He is called by thy name,
For he calls himself a Lamb.
He is meek & he is mild;
He became a little child.
I a child & thou a lamb.
We are called by his name.
   Little Lamb, God bless thee!
   Little Lamb, God bless thee!

The Sick Rose

O Rose, thou art sick!
The invisible worm
That flies in the night,
In the howling storm,

Has found out thy bed
Of crimson joy:
And his dark secret love
Does thy life destroy.

The Tyger

Tyger! Tyger! burning bright
In the forests of the night,
What immortal hand or eye
Could frame thy fearful symmetry?

In what distant deeps or skies
Burnt the fire of thine eyes?
On what wings dare he aspire?
What the hand dare sieze the fire?

And what shoulder, & what art,
Could twist the sinews of thy heart?
And when thy heart began to beat,
What dread hand? & what dread feet?

What the hammer? what the chain?
In what furnace was thy brain?
What the anvil? what dread grasp
Dare its deadly terrors clasp?

When the stars threw down their spears,
And water'd heaven with their tears,
Did he smile his work to see?
Did he who made the Lamb make thee?

Tyger! Tyger! burning bright
In the forests of the night,
What immortal hand or eye
Dare frame thy fearful symmetry?

London

I wander thro' each charter'd street,
Near where the charter'd Thames does flow,
And mark in every face I meet
Marks of weakness, marks of woe.

In every cry of every Man,
In every Infant's cry of fear,

In every voice, in every ban,
The mind-forg'd manacles I hear.

How the Chimney-sweeper's cry
Every black'ning Church appalls;
And the hapless Soldier's sigh
Runs in blood down Palace walls.

But most thro' midnight streets I hear
How the youthful Harlot's curse
Blasts the new born Infant's tear,
And blights with plagues the Marriage hearse.

ROBERT BURNS *(1759–1796)*

The national poet of Scotland, Burns is best known for colorful, often humorous songs and poems written in the dialect of his homeland. Though largely self-educated, Burns was a meticulous craftsman who was a master of complex literary forms.

To a Mouse

On Turning Her up in Her Nest with
the Plough, November, 1785

I   Wee, sleekit, cowrin, tim'rous beastie,
     O, what a panic's in thy breastie!
     Thou need na start awa sae hasty
                    Wi' bickering brattle![1]
     I wad be laith to rin an' chase thee,
                    Wi' murdering pattle![2]

II   I'm truly sorry man's dominion
     Has broken Nature's social union,

---

[1] *bickering brattle*] noisy scamper.
[2] *pattle*] plough-staff.

An' justifies that ill opinion
> Which makes thee startle
At me, thy poor, earth-born companion
> An' fellow mortal!

III   I doubt na, whyles,[3] but thou may thieve;
What then? poor beastie, thou maun live!
A daimen icker in a thrave[4]
> 'S a sma' request;
I'll get a blessin wi' the lave,[5]
> An' never miss 't!

IV   Thy wee-bit housie, too, in ruin!
Its silly wa's the win's are strewin!
An' naething, now, to big[6] a new ane,
> O' foggage[7] green!
An' bleak December's win's ensuin,
> Baith snell[8] an' keen!

V   Thou saw the fields laid bare an' waste,
An' weary winter comin fast,
An' cozie here, beneath the blast,
> Thou thought to dwell,
Till crash! the cruel coulter past
> Out thro' thy cell.

VI   That wee bit heap o' leaves an' stibble,
Has cost thee monie a weary nibble!
Now thou's turned out, for a' thy trouble,
> But house or hald,[9]
To thole[10] the winter's sleety dribble,
> An' cranreuch[11] cauld!

---

[3] *whyles*] sometimes.
[4] *A daimen icker in a thrave*] An occasional ear of corn in 24 sheaves.
[5] *lave*] remainder.
[6] *big*] build.
[7] *foggage*] meadow grass.
[8] *snell*] biting.
[9] *But house or hald*] Without house or property.
[10] *thole*] endure.
[11] *cranreuch*] hoarfrost.

VII   But Mousie, thou art no thy lane,[12]
    In proving foresight may be vain:
    The best-laid schemes o' mice an' men
          Gang aft agley,[13]
    An' lea'e us nought but grief an' pain,
          For promis'd joy!

VIII   Still thou art blest, compared wi' me!
    The present only toucheth thee:
    But och! I backward cast my e'e,
          On prospects drear!
    An' forward, tho' I canna see,
          I guess an' fear!

A Red, Red Rose

I   O, my luve is like a red, red rose,
    That's newly sprung in June.
    O, my luve is like the melodie,
    That's sweetly play'd in tune.

II   As fair art thou, my bonie lass,
    So deep in luve am I,
    And I will luve thee still, my dear,
    Till a' the seas gang dry.

III   Till a' the seas gang dry, my dear,
    And the rocks melt wi' the sun!
    And I will luve thee still, my dear,
    While the sands o' life shall run.

IV   And fare thee weel, my only luve,
    And fare thee weel a while!
    And I will come again, my luve,
    Tho' it were ten thousand mile!

---

[12] *no thy lane*] not alone.
[13] *agley*] awry.

WILLIAM WORDSWORTH *(1770–1850)*

Wordsworth was a pioneering figure of the Romantic movement and is one of English literature's major poets. Although he was viewed in his later life as a symbol of complacency by younger writers, his greatest works are masterpieces of eloquent passion.

Composed upon Westminster Bridge, Sept. 3, 1802

Earth has not anything to show more fair:
Dull would he be of soul who could pass by
A sight so touching in its majesty:
This City now doth, like a garment, wear
The beauty of the morning; silent, bare,
Ships, towers, domes, theatres, and temples lie
Open unto the fields, and to the sky;
All bright and glittering in the smokeless air.
Never did sun more beautifully steep
In his first splendour, valley, rock, or hill;
Ne'er saw I, never felt, a calm so deep!
The river glideth at his own sweet will:
Dear God! the very houses seem asleep;
And all that mighty heart is lying still!

"I Wandered Lonely as a Cloud"

I wandered lonely as a cloud
That floats on high o'er vales and hills,
When all at once I saw a crowd,
A host, of golden daffodils;
Beside the lake, beneath the trees,
Fluttering and dancing in the breeze.

Continuous as the stars that shine
And twinkle on the milky way,
They stretched in never-ending line
Along the margin of a bay:
Ten thousand saw I at a glance,
Tossing their heads in sprightly dance.

The waves beside them danced; but they
Out-did the sparkling waves in glee:
A poet could not but be gay,

In such a jocund company:
I gazed — and gazed — but little thought
What wealth the show to me had brought:

For oft, when on my couch I lie
In vacant or in pensive mood,
They flash upon that inward eye
Which is the bliss of solitude;
And then my heart with pleasure fills,
And dances with the daffodils.

"The World Is Too Much with Us; Late and Soon"

The world is too much with us; late and soon,
Getting and spending, we lay waste our powers:
Little we see in Nature that is ours;
We have given our hearts away, a sordid boon!
The Sea that bares her bosom to the moon;
The winds that will be howling at all hours,
And are up-gathered now like sleeping flowers;
For this, for everything, we are out of tune;
It moves us not. — Great God! I'd rather be
A Pagan suckled in a creed outworn;
So might I, standing on this pleasant lea,
Have glimpses that would make me less forlorn;
Have sight of Proteus rising from the sea;
Or hear old Triton blow his wreathèd horn.

SAMUEL TAYLOR COLERIDGE *(1772–1834)*

A close associate of Wordsworth, Coleridge was similarly one of the leading Roman-
tic poets, as well as an important critic and essayist. His longtime narcotics addiction
gave many of his works a fantastical quality: "Kubla Khan" was admittedly inspired
by an opium dream.

Kubla Khan

In Xanadu did Kubla Khan
A stately pleasure-dome decree:
Where Alph, the sacred river, ran
Through caverns measureless to man

Down to a sunless sea.
So twice five miles of fertile ground
With walls and towers were girdled round:
And there were gardens bright with sinuous rills,
Where blossomed many an incense-bearing tree;
And here were forests ancient as the hills,
Enfolding sunny spots of greenery.

But oh! that deep romantic chasm which slanted
Down the green hill athwart a cedarn cover!
A savage place! as holy and enchanted
As e'er beneath a waning moon was haunted
By woman wailing for her demon-lover!
And from this chasm, with ceaseless turmoil seething,
As if this earth in fast thick pants were breathing,
A mighty fountain momently was forced:
Amid whose swift half-intermitted burst
Huge fragments vaulted like rebounding hail,
Or chaffy grain beneath the thresher's flail:
And 'mid these dancing rocks at once and ever
It flung up momently the sacred river.
Five miles meandering with a mazy motion
Through wood and dale the sacred river ran,
Then reached the caverns measureless to man,
And sank in tumult to a lifeless ocean:
And 'mid this tumult Kubla heard from far
Ancestral voices prophesying war!
  The shadow of the dome of pleasure
  Floated midway on the waves;
  Where was heard the mingled measure
  From the fountain and the caves.
It was a miracle of rare device,
A sunny pleasure-dome with caves of ice!

  A damsel with a dulcimer
  In a vision once I saw:
  It was an Abyssinian maid,
  And on her dulcimer she played,
  Singing of Mount Abora.
  Could I revive within me
  Her symphony and song,
  To such a deep delight 'twould win me,
That with music loud and long,

I would build that dome in air,
That sunny dome! those caves of ice!
And all who heard should see them there,
And all should cry, Beware! Beware!
His flashing eyes, his floating hair!
Weave a circle round him thrice,
And close your eyes with holy dread,
For he on honey-dew hath fed,
And drunk the milk of Paradise.

LEIGH HUNT *(1784–1859)*

Better remembered today as an associate of Byron, Shelley and Keats than as a literary original, Hunt was a crusading London journalist notably active in labor reform circles. These two poems, however, have long enjoyed great popularity.

Abou Ben Adhem

Abou Ben Adhem (may his tribe increase!)
Awoke one night from a deep dream of peace,
And saw, within the moonlight in his room,
Making it rich, and like a lily in bloom,
An angel writing in a book of gold: —
Exceeding peace had made Ben Adhem bold,
And to the presence in the room he said,
    "What writest thou?" — The vision rais'd its head,
And with a look made of all sweet accord,
Answer'd, "The names of those who love the Lord."
    "And is mine one?" asked Abou. "Nay, not so,"
Replied the angel. Abou spoke more low,
But cheerly still; and said, "I pray thee, then,
Write me as one that loves his fellow men."

    The angel wrote, and vanish'd. The next night
It came again with a great wakening light,
And show'd the names whom love of God had blest,
And lo! Ben Adhem's name led all the rest.

Jenny Kiss'd Me

Jenny kiss'd me when we met,
   Jumping from the chair she sat in;
Time, you thief, who love to get
   Sweets into your list, put that in!
Say I'm weary, say I'm sad,
   Say that health and wealth have miss'd me,
Say I'm growing old, but add,
   Jenny kiss'd me.

GEORGE GORDON, LORD BYRON (1788–1824)

The prototypical Romantic figure, as well known to contemporaries for his heroic and scandalous personal life as for his writings, Byron continues to represent tempestuous and contradictory qualities of genius, melancholy, courage, despair and passion.

"She Walks in Beauty"

She walks in beauty, like the night
   Of cloudless climes and starry skies;
And all that's best of dark and bright
   Meet in her aspect and her eyes:
Thus mellow'd to that tender light
   Which heaven to gaudy day denies.

One shade the more, one ray the less,
   Had half impair'd the nameless grace
Which waves in every raven tress,
   Or softly lightens o'er her face;
Where thoughts serenely sweet express
   How pure, how dear their dwelling-place.

And on that cheek, and o'er that brow,
   So soft, so calm, yet eloquent,
The smiles that win, the tints that glow,
   But tell of days in goodness spent,
A mind at peace with all below,
   A heart whose love is innocent!

The Destruction of Sennacherib

The Assyrian came down like the wolf on the fold,
And his cohorts were gleaming in purple and gold;
And the sheen of their spears was like stars on the sea,
When the blue wave rolls nightly on deep Galilee.

Like the leaves of the forest when Summer is green,
That host with their banners at sunset were seen:
Like the leaves of the forest when Autumn hath blown,
That host on the morrow lay wither'd and strown.

For the Angel of Death spread his wings on the blast,
And breathed in the face of the foe as he pass'd;
And the eyes of the sleepers wax'd deadly and chill,
And their hearts but once heaved, and for ever grew still!

And there lay the steed with his nostril all wide,
But through it there roll'd not the breath of his pride:
And the foam of his gasping lay white on the turf,
And cold as the spray of the rock-beating surf.

And there lay the rider distorted and pale,
With the dew on his brow and the rust on his mail;
And the tents were all silent, the banners alone,
The lances unlifted, the trumpet unblown.

And the widows of Ashur are loud in their wajl,
And the idols are broke in the temple of Baal;
And the might of the Gentile, unsmote by the sword,
Hath melted like snow in the glance of the Lord!

"So We'll Go No More a Roving"

So we'll go no more a roving
   So late into the night,
Though the heart be still as loving,
   And the moon be still as bright.

For the sword outwears its sheath,
   And the soul wears out the breast,
And the heart must pause to breathe,
   And Love itself have rest.

Though the night was made for loving,
  And the day returns too soon,
Yet we'll go no more a roving
  By the light of the moon.

PERCY BYSSHE SHELLEY (1792–1822)

Shelley was, like his friend Byron, a somewhat larger-than-life Romantic who embodied — as well as helped determine — the rebellious spirit of his era. By the time of his death by drowning at age 29 he had composed a body of work of unequaled range.

Ozymandias

I met a traveller from an antique land
Who said: Two vast and trunkless legs of stone
Stand in the desert . . . Near them, on the sand,
Half sunk, a shattered visage lies, whose frown,
And wrinkled lip, and sneer of cold command,
Tell that its sculptor well those passions read
Which yet survive, stamped on these lifeless things,
The hand that mocked them, and the heart that fed:
And on the pedestal these words appear:
"My name is Ozymandias, king of kings:
Look on my works, ye Mighty, and despair!"
Nothing beside remains. Round the decay
Of that colossal wreck, boundless and bare
The lone and level sands stretch far away.

Ode to the West Wind

I O wild West Wind, thou breath of Autumn's being,
    Thou, from whose unseen presence the leaves dead
    Are driven, like ghosts from an enchanter fleeing,

    Yellow, and black, and pale, and hectic red,
    Pestilence-stricken multitudes: O thou,
    Who chariotest to their dark wintry bed

    The wingèd seeds, where they lie cold and low,
    Each like a corpse within its grave, until
    Thine azure sister of the Spring shall blow

Her clarion o'er the dreaming earth, and fill
(Driving sweet buds like flocks to feed in air)
With living hues and odours plain and hill:

Wild Spirit, which art moving everywhere;
Destroyer and preserver; hear, oh, hear!

II   Thou on whose stream, mid the steep sky's commotion,
Loose clouds like earth's decaying leaves are shed,
Shook from the tangled boughs of Heaven and Ocean,

Angels of rain and lightning: there are spread
On the blue surface of thine aëry surge,
Like the bright hair uplifted from the head

Of some fierce Maenad, even from the dim verge
Of the horizon to the zenith's height,
The locks of the approaching storm. Thou dirge

Of the dying year, to which this closing night
Will be the dome of a vast sepulchre,
Vaulted with all thy congregated might

Of vapours, from whose solid atmosphere
Black rain, and fire, and hail will burst: oh, hear!

III   Thou who didst waken from his summer dreams
The blue Mediterranean, where he lay,
Lulled by the coil of his crystàlline streams,

Beside a pumice isle in Baiae's bay,
And saw in sleep old palaces and towers
Quivering within the wave's intenser day,

All overgrown with azure moss and flowers
So sweet, the sense faints picturing them! Thou
For whose path the Atlantic's level powers

Cleave themselves into chasms, while far below
The sea-blooms and the oozy woods which wear
The sapless foliage of the ocean, know

Thy voice, and suddenly grow gray with fear,
And tremble and despoil themselves: oh, hear!

IV   If I were a dead leaf thou mightest bear;
If I were a swift cloud to fly with thee;
A wave to pant beneath thy power, and share

The impulse of thy strength, only less free
Than thou, O uncontrollable! If even
I were as in my boyhood, and could be

The comrade of thy wanderings over Heaven,
As then, when to outstrip thy skiey speed
Scarce seemed a vision; I would ne'er have striven

As thus with thee in prayer in my sore need.
Oh, lift me as a wave, a leaf, a cloud!
I fall upon the thorns of life! I bleed!

A heavy weight of hours has chained and bowed
One too like thee: tameless, and swift, and proud.

v   Make me thy lyre, even as the forest is:
What if my leaves are falling like its own!
The tumult of thy mighty harmonies

Will take from both a deep, autumnal tone,
Sweet though in sadness. Be thou, Spirit fierce,
My spirit! Be thou me, impetuous one!

Drive my dead thoughts over the universe
Like withered leaves to quicken a new birth!
And, by the incantation of this verse,

Scatter, as from an unextinguished hearth
Ashes and sparks, my words among mankind!
Be through my lips to unawakened earth

The trumpet of a prophecy! O, Wind,
If Winter comes, can Spring be far behind?

To a Skylark

Hail to thee, blithe Spirit!
   Bird thou never wert,
That from Heaven, or near it,
   Pourest thy full heart
In profuse strains of unpremeditated art.

Higher still and higher
   From the earth thou springest
Like a cloud of fire;
   The blue deep thou wingest,
And singing still dost soar, and soaring ever singest.

In the golden lightning
    Of the sunken sun,
O'er which clouds are bright'ning,
    Thou dost float and run;
Like an unbodied joy whose race is just begun.

The pale purple even
    Melts around thy flight;
Like a star of Heaven,
    In the broad daylight
Thou art unseen, but yet I hear thy shrill delight,

Keen as are the arrows
    Of that silver sphere,
Whose intense lamp narrows
    In the white dawn clear
Until we hardly see — we feel that it is there.

All the earth and air
    With thy voice is loud,
As, when night is bare,
    From one lonely cloud
The moon rains out her beams, and Heaven is overflowed.

What thou art we know not;
    What is most like thee?
From rainbow clouds there flow not
    Drops so bright to see
As from thy presence showers a rain of melody.

Like a Poet hidden
    In the light of thought,
Singing hymns unbidden,
    Till the world is wrought
To sympathy with hopes and fears it heeded not:

Like a high-born maiden
    In a palace-tower,
Soothing her love-laden
    Soul in secret hour
With music sweet as love, which overflows her bower:

Like a glow-worm golden
    In a dell of dew,
Scattering unbeholden

   Its aëreal hue
Among the flowers and grass, which screen it from the view!

   Like a rose embowered
    In its own green leaves,
   By warm winds deflowered,
    Till the scent it gives
Makes faint with too much sweet those heavy-wingèd thieves:

   Sound of vernal showers
    On the twinkling grass,
   Rain-awakened flowers,
    All that ever was
Joyous, and clear, and fresh, thy music doth surpass:

   Teach us, Sprite or Bird,
    What sweet thoughts are thine:
   I have never heard
    Praise of love or wine
That panted forth a flood of rapture so divine.

   Chorus Hymeneal,
    Or triumphal chant,
   Matched with thine would be all
    But an empty vaunt,
A thing wherein we feel there is some hidden want.

   What objects are the fountains
    Of thy happy strain?
   What fields, or waves, or mountains?
    What shapes of sky or plain?
What love of thine own kind? what ignorance of pain?

   With thy clear keen joyance
    Languor cannot be:
   Shadow of annoyance
    Never came near thee:
Thou lovest—but ne'er knew love's sad satiety.

   Waking or asleep,
    Thou of death must deem
   Things more true and deep
    Than we mortals dream,
Or how could thy notes flow in such a crystal stream?

We look before and after,
　　And pine for what is not:
Our sincerest laughter
　　With some pain is fraught;
Our sweetest songs are those that tell of saddest thought.

Yet if we could scorn
　　Hate, and pride, and fear;
If we were things born
　　Not to shed a tear,
I know not how thy joy we ever should come near.

Better than all measures
　　Of delightful sound,
Better than all treasures
　　That in books are found,
Thy skill to poet were, thou scorner of the ground!

Teach me half the gladness
　　That thy brain must know,
Such harmonious madness
　　From my lips would flow
The world should listen then — as I am listening now.

WILLIAM CULLEN BRYANT *(1794–1878)*

As editor of the New York *Evening Post*, Bryant was one of the most respected journalists of his day as well as a widely read poet and essayist. He composed the first draft of "Thanatopsis" when only seventeen years old.

Thanatopsis

To him who in the love of nature holds
Communion with her visible forms, she speaks
A various language; for his gayer hours
She has a voice of gladness, and a smile
And eloquence of beauty, and she glides
Into his darker musings, with a mild
And gentle sympathy, that steals away
Their sharpness, ere he is aware. When thoughts
Of the last bitter hour come like a blight
Over thy spirit, and sad images

Of the stern agony, and shroud, and pall,
And breathless darkness, and the narrow house,
Make thee to shudder, and grow sick at heart; —
Go forth, under the open sky, and list
To Nature's teachings, while from all around —
Earth and her waters, and the depths of air, —
Comes a still voice — Yet a few days, and thee
The all-beholding sun shall see no more
In all his course; nor yet in the cold ground,
Where thy pale form was laid, with many tears,
Nor in the embrace of ocean shall exist
Thy image. Earth, that nourished thee, shall claim
Thy growth, to be resolved to earth again;
And, lost each human trace, surrendering up
Thine individual being, shalt thou go
To mix forever with the elements,
To be a brother to the insensible rock
And to the sluggish clod, which the rude swain
Turns with his share, and treads upon. The oak
Shall send his roots abroad, and pierce thy mould.
Yet not to thy eternal resting place
Shalt thou retire alone — nor couldst thou wish
Couch more magnificent. Thou shalt lie down
With patriarchs of the infant world — with kings,
The powerful of the earth — the wise, the good,
Fair forms, and hoary seers of ages past,
All in one mighty sepulchre. — The hills
Rock-ribbed and ancient as the sun, — the vales
Stretching in pensive quietness between;
The venerable woods — rivers that move
In majesty, and the complaining brooks
That make the meadows green; and poured round all,
Old ocean's gray and melancholy waste, —
Are but the solemn decorations all
Of the great tomb of man. The golden sun,
The planets, all the infinite host of heaven,
Are shining on the sad abodes of death,
Through the still lapse of ages. All that tread
The globe are but a handful to the tribes
That slumber in its bosom. — Take the wings
Of morning — and the Barcan desert pierce,
Or lose thyself in the continuous woods

Where rolls the Oregan, and hears no sound,
Save his own dashings — yet — the dead are there,
And millions in those solitudes, since first
The flight of years began, have laid them down
In their last sleep — the dead reign there alone.
So shalt thou rest — and what if thou shalt fall
Unheeded by the living — and no friend
Take note of thy departure? All that breathe
Will share thy destiny. The gay will laugh
When thou art gone, the solemn brood of care
Plod on, and each one as before will chase
His favorite phantom; yet all these shall leave
Their mirth and their employments, and shall come,
And make their bed with thee. As the long train
Of ages glide away, the sons of men,
The youth in life's green spring, and he who goes
In the full strength of years, matron, and maid,
And the sweet babe, and the gray-headed man, —
Shall one by one be gathered to thy side,
By those, who in their turn shall follow them.
So live, that when thy summons comes to join
The innumerable caravan, that moves
To that mysterious realm, where each shall take
His chamber in the silent halls of death,
Thou go not, like the quarry-slave at night,
Scourged to his dungeon, but sustained and soothed
By an unfaltering trust, approach thy grave,
Like one who wraps the drapery of his couch
About him, and lies down to pleasant dreams.

JOHN KEATS *(1795–1821)*

In his short life Keats developed a distinctive poetic style of precocious maturity. His poetry and letters contain profound insights into the nature of beauty, art, suffering, mortality and other perennial issues.

On First Looking into Chapman's Homer

Much have I travell'd in the realms of gold,
  And many goodly states and kingdoms seen;
  Round many western islands have I been

Which bards in fealty to Apollo hold.
Oft of one wide expanse had I been told
   That deep-brow'd Homer ruled as his demesne;
   Yet did I never breathe its pure serene
Till I heard Chapman[1] speak out loud and bold:
Then felt I like some watcher of the skies
   When a new planet swims into his ken;
Or like stout Cortez when with eagle eyes
   He star'd at the Pacific — and all his men
Look'd at each other with a wild surmise —
   Silent, upon a peak in Darien.

Ode to a Nightingale

I   My heart aches, and a drowsy numbness pains
     My sense, as though of hemlock I had drunk,
   Or emptied some dull opiate to the drains
     One minute past, and Lethe-wards had sunk:
'Tis not through envy of thy happy lot,
     But being too happy in thine happiness, —
       That thou, light-winged Dryad of the trees,
         In some melodious plot
   Of beechen green, and shadows numberless,
       Singest of summer in full-throated ease.

II   O, for a draught of vintage! that hath been
     Cool'd a long age in the deep-delved earth,
   Tasting of Flora and the country green,
     Dance, and Provençal song, and sunburnt mirth!
O for a beaker full of the warm South,
     Full of the true, the blushful Hippocrene,
       With beaded bubbles winking at the brim,
         And purple-stained mouth;
   That I might drink, and leave the world unseen,
       And with thee fade away into the forest dim:

III   Fade far away, dissolve, and quite forget
     What thou among the leaves hast never known,
   The weariness, the fever, and the fret

---

[1] *Chapman*] George Chapman (c. 1559–1634), Elizabethan poet famed for his transla-
tions of the epic poems of Homer.

Here, where men sit and hear each other groan;
Where palsy shakes a few, sad, last gray hairs,
   Where youth grows pale, and spectre-thin, and dies;
     Where but to think is to be full of sorrow
       And leaden-eyed despairs,
  Where Beauty cannot keep her lustrous eyes,
    Or new Love pine at them beyond to-morrow.

IV   Away! away! for I will fly to thee,
    Not charioted by Bacchus and his pards,
But on the viewless wings of Poesy,
    Though the dull brain perplexes and retards:
Already with thee! tender is the night,
    And haply the Queen-Moon is on her throne,
       Cluster'd around by all her starry Fays;
         But here there is no light,
    Save what from heaven is with the breezes blown
      Through verdurous glooms and winding mossy ways.

V   I cannot see what flowers are at my feet,
    Nor what soft incense hangs upon the boughs,
But, in embalmed darkness, guess each sweet
    Wherewith the seasonable month endows
The grass, the thicket, and the fruit-tree wild;
    White hawthorn, and the pastoral eglantine;
       Fast fading violets cover'd up in leaves;
         And mid-May's eldest child,
    The coming musk-rose, full of dewy wine,
      The murmurous haunt of flies on summer eves.

VI   Darkling I listen; and, for many a time
    I have been half in love with easeful Death,
Call'd him soft names in many a mused rhyme,
    To take into the air my quiet breath;
Now more than ever seems it rich to die,
    To cease upon the midnight with no pain,
       While thou art pouring forth thy soul abroad
         In such an ecstasy!
    Still wouldst thou sing, and I have ears in vain —
      To thy high requiem become a sod.

VII   Thou wast not born for death, immortal Bird!
        No hungry generations tread thee down;
    The voice I hear this passing night was heard
        In ancient days by emperor and clown:
    Perhaps the self-same song that found a path
        Through the sad heart of Ruth, when, sick for home,
          She stood in tears amid the alien corn;
            The same that oft-times hath
        Charm'd magic casements, opening on the foam
        Of perilous seas, in faery lands forlorn.

VIII   Forlorn! the very word is like a bell
        To toll me back from thee to my sole self!
    Adieu! the fancy cannot cheat so well
        As she is fam'd to do, deceiving elf.
    Adieu! adieu! thy plaintive anthem fades
        Past the near meadows, over the still stream,
          Up the hill-side; and now 'tis buried deep
            In the next valley-glades:
        Was it a vision, or a waking dream?
          Fled is that music: — Do I wake or sleep?

Ode on a Grecian Urn

I   Thou still unravish'd bride of quietness,
        Thou foster-child of silence and slow time,
    Sylvan historian, who canst thus express
        A flowery tale more sweetly than our rhyme:
    What leaf-fring'd legend haunts about thy shape
        Of deities or mortals, or of both,
          In Tempe or the dales of Arcady?
        What men or gods are these? What maidens loth?
    What mad pursuit? What struggle to escape?
        What pipes and timbrels? What wild ecstasy?

II   Heard melodies are sweet, but those unheard
        Are sweeter; therefore, ye soft pipes, play on;
    Not to the sensual ear, but, more endear'd,
        Pipe to the spirit ditties of no tone:

Fair youth, beneath the trees, thou canst not leave
  Thy song, nor ever can those trees be bare;
    Bold Lover, never, never canst thou kiss,
Though winning near the goal — yet, do not grieve;
  She cannot fade, though thou hast not thy bliss,
    For ever wilt thou love, and she be fair!

III Ah, happy, happy boughs! that cannot shed
    Your leaves, nor ever bid the Spring adieu;
  And, happy melodist, unwearied,
    For ever piping songs for ever new;
  More happy love! more happy, happy love!
    For ever warm and still to be enjoy'd,
      For ever panting, and for ever young;
  All breathing human passion far above,
    That leaves a heart high-sorrowful and cloy'd,
      A burning forehead, and a parching tongue.

IV Who are these coming to the sacrifice?
    To what green altar, O mysterious priest,
  Lead'st thou that heifer lowing at the skies,
    And all her silken flanks with garlands drest?
  What little town by river or sea shore,
    Or mountain-built with peaceful citadel,
      Is emptied of this folk, this pious morn?
  And, little town, thy streets for evermore
    Will silent be; and not a soul to tell
      Why thou art desolate, can e'er return.

V O Attic shape! Fair attitude! with brede
    Of marble men and maidens overwrought,
  With forest branches and the trodden weed;
    Thou, silent form, dost tease us out of thought
  As doth eternity: Cold Pastoral!
    When old age shall this generation waste,
      Thou shalt remain, in midst of other woe
  Than ours, a friend to man, to whom thou say'st,
    "Beauty is truth, truth beauty," — that is all
      Ye know on earth, and all ye need to know.

La Belle Dame sans Merci

A BALLAD

I   O, what can ail thee, knight-at-arms,
      Alone and palely loitering?
    The sedge has wither'd from the lake,
      And no birds sing.

II   O, what can ail thee, knight-at-arms,
      So haggard and so woe-begone?
    The squirrel's granary is full,
      And the harvest's done.

III   I see a lilly on thy brow,
      With anguish moist and fever dew;
    And on thy cheeks a fading rose
      Fast withereth too.

IV   I met a lady in the meads,
      Full beautiful — a faery's child,
    Her hair was long, her foot was light,
      And her eyes were wild.

V   I made a garland for her head,
      And bracelets too, and fragrant zone;
    She look'd at me as she did love,
      And made sweet moan.

VI   I set her on my pacing steed,
      And nothing else saw all day long;
    For sidelong would she bend, and sing
      A faery's song.

VII   She found me roots of relish sweet,
      And honey wild, and manna dew,
    And sure in language strange she said —
      "I love thee true."

VIII   She took me to her elfin grot,
      And there she wept and sigh'd full sore,
    And there I shut her wild wild eyes
      With kisses four.

IX   And there she lulled me asleep
          And there I dream'd — Ah! woe betide!
      The latest dream I ever dream'd
          On the cold hill side.

X   I saw pale kings and princes too,
          Pale warriors, death-pale were they all;
      They cried — "La Belle Dame sans Merci
          Hath thee in thrall!"

XI   I saw their starved lips in the gloam,
          With horrid warning gaped wide,
      And I awoke and found me here,
          On the cold hill's side.

XII   And this is why I sojourn here
          Alone and palely loitering,
      Though the sedge has wither'd from the lake,
          And no birds sing.

"When I Have Fears That I May Cease to Be"

When I have fears that I may cease to be
   Before my pen has glean'd my teeming brain,
Before high-piled books, in charactery,
   Hold like rich garners the full ripen'd grain;
When I behold, upon the night's starr'd face,
   Huge cloudy symbols of a high romance,
And think that I may never live to trace
   Their shadows, with the magic hand of chance;
And when I feel, fair creature of an hour,
   That I shall never look upon thee more,
Never have relish in the faery power
   Of unreflecting love; — then on the shore
Of the wide world I stand alone, and think
Till love and fame to nothingness do sink.

RALPH WALDO EMERSON *(1803–1882)*

One of the essential figures of American literature, Emerson is associated with the Transcendentalist group of philosophical idealists. Best known for his essays, he also wrote prolifically in verse; "Concord Hymn" was long a staple of the American classroom.

Hymn: Sung at the Completion of the Concord Monument

APRIL 19, 1836

By the rude bridge that arched the flood,
   Their flag to April's breeze unfurled,
Here once the embattled farmers stood,
   And fired the shot heard round the world.

The foe long since in silence slept;
   Alike the conqueror silent sleeps;
And Time the ruined bridge has swept
   Down the dark stream which seaward creeps.

On this green bank, by this soft stream,
   We set to-day a votive stone;
That memory may their deed redeem,
   When, like our sires, our sons are gone.

Spirit, that made those heroes dare
   To die, or leave their children free,
Bid Time and Nature gently spare
   The shaft we raise to them and thee.

ELIZABETH BARRETT BROWNING *(1806–1861)*

The most famous female English poet of her day, Browning was married to poet Robert Browning, for whom she wrote the famous sonnet sequence *Sonnets from the Portuguese*, the romantic themes of which are embodied in the following selection.

Sonnet XLIII

How do I love thee? Let me count the ways.
I love thee to the depth and breadth and height
My soul can reach, when feeling out of sight

For the ends of Being and ideal Grace.
I love thee to the level of everyday's
Most quiet need, by sun and candle-light.
I love thee freely, as men strive for Right;
I love thee purely, as they turn from Praise.
I love thee with the passion put to use
In my old griefs, and with my childhood's faith.
I love thee with a love I seemed to lose
With my lost saints, — I love thee with the breath,
Smiles, tears, of all my life! — and, if God choose,
I shall but love thee better after death.

HENRY WADSWORTH LONGFELLOW *(1807–1882)*

The most popular American poet of the nineteenth century, Longfellow is well
remembered for works such as "Paul Revere's Ride" and "The Song of Hiawatha."
Two of his most famous shorter poems follow.

The Village Blacksmith

Under a spreading chestnut tree
    The village smithy stands;
The smith, a mighty man is he,
    With large and sinewy hands;
And the muscles of his brawny arms
    Are strong as iron bands.

His hair is crisp, and black, and long,
    His face is like the tan;
His brow is wet with honest sweat,
    He earns whate'er he can,
And looks the whole world in the face,
    For he owes not any man.

Week in, week out, from morn till night,
    You can hear his bellows blow;
You can hear him swing his heavy sledge,
    With measured beat and slow,
Like a sexton ringing the village bell,
    When the evening sun is low.

And children coming home from school
　　Look in at the open door;
They love to see the flaming forge,
　　And hear the bellows roar,
And catch the burning sparks that fly
　　Like chaff from a threshing floor.

He goes on Sunday to the church,
　　And sits among his boys;
He hears the parson pray and preach,
　　He hears his daughter's voice,
Singing in the village choir,
　　And it makes his heart rejoice.

It sounds to him like her mother's voice,
　　Singing in Paradise!
He needs must think of her once more,
　　How in the grave she lies;
And with his hard, rough hand he wipes
　　A tear out of his eyes.

Toiling, — rejoicing, — sorrowing,
　　Onward through life he goes;
Each morning sees some task begin,
　　Each evening sees it close;
Something attempted, something done,
　　Has earned a night's repose.

Thanks, thanks to thee, my worthy friend,
　　For the lesson thou hast taught!
Thus at the flaming forge of life
　　Our fortunes must be wrought;
Thus on its sounding anvil shaped
　　Each burning deed and thought!

The Children's Hour

Between the dark and the daylight,
　　When the night is beginning to lower,
Comes a pause in the day's occupations,
　　That is known as the Children's Hour.

I hear in the chamber above me
 The patter of little feet,
The sound of a door that is opened,
 And voices soft and sweet.

From my study I see in the lamplight,
 Descending the broad hall stair,
Grave Alice, and laughing Allegra,
 And Edith with golden hair.

A whisper, and then a silence:
 Yet I know by their merry eyes
They are plotting and planning together
 To take me by surprise.

A sudden rush from the stairway,
 A sudden raid from the hall!
By three doors left unguarded
 They enter my castle wall!

They climb up into my turret
 O'er the arms and back of my chair;
If I try to escape, they surround me;
 They seem to be everywhere.

They almost devour me with kisses,
 Their arms about me entwine,
Till I think of the Bishop of Bingen
 In his Mouse-Tower on the Rhine!

Do you think, O blue-eyed banditti,
 Because you have scaled the wall,
Such an old moustache as I am
 Is not a match for you all!

I have you fast in my fortress,
 And will not let you depart,
But put you down into the dungeon
 In the round-tower of my heart.

And there will I keep you forever,
 Yes, forever and a day,
Till the walls shall crumble to ruin,
 And moulder in dust away!

JOHN GREENLEAF WHITTIER *(1807–1892)*

A Quaker active in the Abolition movement, Whittier was one of the most popular and prolific American poets of the nineteenth century. "Barbara Frietchie" is loosely based on an actual Civil War episode.

Barbara Frietchie

Up from the meadows rich with corn,
Clear in the cool September morn,

The clustered spires of Frederick stand
Green-walled by the hills of Maryland.

Round about them orchards sweep,
Apple- and peach-tree fruited deep,

Fair as a garden of the Lord
To the eyes of the famished rebel horde,

On that pleasant morn of the early fall
When Lee marched over the mountain wall, —

Over the mountains winding down,
Horse and foot, into Frederick town.

Forty flags with their silver stars,
Forty flags with their crimson bars,

Flapped in the morning wind: the sun
Of noon looked down, and saw not one.

Up rose old Barbara Frietchie then,
Bowed with her fourscore years and ten;

Bravest of all in Frederick town,
She took up the flag the men hauled down;

In her attic-window the staff she set,
To show that one heart was loyal yet.

Up the street came the rebel tread,
Stonewall Jackson riding ahead.

Under his slouched hat left and right
He glanced: the old flag met his sight.

"Halt!" — the dust-brown ranks stood fast.
"Fire!" — out blazed the rifle-blast.

It shivered the window, pane and sash;
It rent the banner with seam and gash.

Quick, as it fell, from the broken staff
Dame Barbara snatched the silken scarf;

She leaned far out on the window-sill,
And shook it forth with a royal will.

"Shoot, if you must, this old gray head,
But spare your country's flag," she said.

A shade of sadness, a blush of shame,
Over the face of the leader came;

The nobler nature within him stirred
To life at that woman's deed and word:

"Who touches a hair of yon gray head
Dies like a dog! March on!" he said.

All day long through Frederick street
Sounded the tread of marching feet:

All day long that free flag tost
Over the heads of the rebel host.

Ever its torn folds rose and fell
On the loyal winds that loved it well;

And through the hill-gaps sunset light
Shone over it with a warm good-night.

Barbara Frietchie's work is o'er,
And the Rebel rides on his raids no more.

Honor to her! and let a tear
Fall, for her sake, on Stonewall's bier.

Over Barbara Frietchie's grave
Flag of Freedom and Union, wave!

Peace and order and beauty draw
Round thy symbol of light and law;

And ever the stars above look down
On thy stars below in Frederick town!

EDGAR ALLAN POE *(1809–1849)*

Although he is today most widely recognized as the author of tales of horror and mystery, Poe also wrote poems that have been widely appreciated for their mixture of melancholy Romanticism, musical cadence and fantastical imagery.

To Helen

Helen, thy beauty is to me
   Like those Nicéan barks of yore,
That gently, o'er a perfumed sea,
   The weary, way-worn wanderer bore
   To his own native shore.

On desperate seas long wont to roam,
   Thy hyacinth hair, thy classic face,
Thy Naiad airs have brought me home
   To the glory that was Greece,
   And the grandeur that was Rome.

Lo! in yon brilliant window-niche
   How statue-like I see thee stand,
The agate lamp within thy hand!
   Ah, Psyche, from the regions which
   Are Holy-Land!

The Raven

Once upon a midnight dreary, while I pondered, weak and weary,
Over many a quaint and curious volume of forgotten lore —
While I nodded, nearly napping, suddenly there came a tapping,
As of some one gently rapping, rapping at my chamber door.
" 'Tis some visiter," I muttered, "tapping at my chamber door —
                    Only this and nothing more."

Ah, distinctly I remember it was in the bleak December;
And each separate dying ember wrought its ghost upon the floor.
Eagerly I wished the morrow; — vainly I had sought to borrow
From my books surcease of sorrow — sorrow for the lost Lenore —
For the rare and radiant maiden whom the angels name Lenore —
                    Nameless *here* for evermore.

And the silken, sad, uncertain rustling of each purple curtain
Thrilled me — filled me with fantastic terrors never felt before;

So that now, to still the beating of my heart, I stood repeating
" 'Tis some visiter entreating entrance at my chamber door —
Some late visiter entreating entrance at my chamber door; —
                            This it is and nothing more."

Presently my soul grew stronger; hesitating then no longer,
"Sir," said I, "or Madam, truly your forgiveness I implore;
But the fact is I was napping, and so gently you came rapping,
And so faintly you came tapping, tapping at my chamber door,
That I scarce was sure I heard you" — here I opened wide the
    door; ——
                            Darkness there and nothing more.

Deep into that darkness peering, long I stood there wondering,
    fearing,
Doubting, dreaming dreams no mortal ever dared to dream before;
But the silence was unbroken, and the stillness gave no token,
And the only word there spoken was the whispered word,
    "Lenore?"
This I whispered, and an echo murmured back the word,
    "Lenore!"
                            Merely this and nothing more.

Back into the chamber turning, all my soul within me burning,
Soon again I heard a tapping somewhat louder than before.
"Surely," said I, "surely that is something at my window lattice;
Let me see, then, what thereat is, and this mystery explore —
Let my heart be still a moment and this mystery explore; —
                            'Tis the wind and nothing more!"

Open here I flung the shutter, when, with many a flirt and flutter,
In there stepped a stately Raven of the saintly days of yore;
Not the least obeisance made he; not a minute stopped or stayed
    he;
But, with mien of lord or lady, perched above my chamber door —
Perched upon a bust of Pallas just above my chamber door —
                            Perched, and sat, and nothing more.

Then this ebony bird beguiling my sad fancy into smiling,
By the grave and stern decorum of the countenance it wore,
"Though thy crest be shorn and shaven, thou," I said, "art sure no
    craven,

Ghastly grim and ancient Raven wandering from the Nightly
  shore —
Tell me what thy lordly name is on the Night's Plutonian shore!"
                          Quoth the Raven "Nevermore."

Much I marvelled this ungainly fowl to hear discourse so plainly,
Though its answer little meaning — little relevancy bore;
For we cannot help agreeing that no living human being
Ever yet was blessed with seeing bird above his chamber door —
Bird or beast upon the sculptured bust above his chamber door,
                          With such name as "Nevermore."

But the Raven, sitting lonely on the placid bust, spoke only
That one word, as if his soul in that one word he did outpour.
Nothing farther then he uttered — not a feather then he fluttered —
Till I scarcely more than muttered "Other friends have flown
  before —
On the morrow *he* will leave me, as my Hopes have flown before."
                          Then the bird said "Nevermore."

Startled at the stillness broken by reply so aptly spoken,
"Doubtless," said I, "what it utters is its only stock and store
Caught from some unhappy master whom unmerciful Disaster
Followed fast and followed faster till his songs one burden bore —
Till the dirges of his Hope that melancholy burden bore
                          Of 'Never — nevermore.' "

But the Raven still beguiling my sad fancy into smiling,
Straight I wheeled a cushioned seat in front of bird, and bust and
  door;
Then, upon the velvet sinking, I betook myself to linking
Fancy unto fancy, thinking what this ominous bird of yore —
What this grim, ungainly, ghastly, gaunt, and ominous bird of yore
                          Meant in croaking "Nevermore."

This I sat engaged in guessing, but no syllable expressing
To the fowl whose fiery eyes now burned into my bosom's core;
This and more I sat divining, with my head at ease reclining
On the cushion's velvet lining that the lamp-light gloated o'er,
But whose velvet-violet lining with the lamp-light gloating o'er,
                          She shall press, ah, nevermore!

Then, methought, the air grew denser, perfumed from an unseen
  censer
Swung by seraphim whose foot-falls tinkled on the tufted floor.

"Wretch," I cried, "thy God hath lent thee — by these angels he
    hath sent thee
Respite — respite and nepenthe from thy memories of Lenore;
Quaff, oh quaff this kind nepenthe and forget this lost Lenore!"
                                Quoth the Raven "Nevermore."

"Prophet!" said I, "thing of evil! — prophet still, if bird or devil! —
Whether Tempter sent, or whether tempest tossed thee here
    ashore,
Desolate yet all undaunted, on this desert land enchanted —
On this home by Horror haunted — tell me truly, I implore —
Is there — *is* there balm in Gilead? — tell me — tell me, I implore!"
                                Quoth the Raven "Nevermore."

"Prophet!" said I, "thing of evil! — prophet still, if bird or devil!
By that Heaven that bends above us — by that God we both
    adore —
Tell this soul with sorrow laden if, within the distant Aidenn,
It shall clasp a sainted maiden whom the angels name Lenore —
Clasp a rare and radiant maiden whom the angels name Lenore."
                                Quoth the Raven "Nevermore."

"Be that word our sign of parting, bird or fiend!" I shrieked,
    upstarting —
"Get thee back into the tempest and the Night's Plutonian shore!
Leave no black plume as a token of that lie thy soul hath spoken!
Leave my loneliness unbroken! — quit the bust above my door!
Take thy beak from out my heart, and take thy form from off my
    door!"
                                Quoth the Raven "Nevermore."

And the Raven, never flitting, still is sitting, *still* is sitting
On the pallid bust of Pallas just above my chamber door;
And his eyes have all the seeming of a demon's that is dreaming,
And the lamp-light o'er him streaming throws his shadow on the
    floor;
And my soul from out that shadow that lies floating on the floor
                                Shall be lifted — nevermore!

Annabel Lee

It was many and many a year ago,
    In a kingdom by the sea,
That a maiden there lived whom you may know

By the name of Annabel Lee; —
And this maiden she lived with no other thought
    Than to love and be loved by me.

She was a child and *I* was a child,
    In this kingdom by the sea,
But we loved with a love that was more than love —
    I and my Annabel Lee —
With a love that the wingéd seraphs of Heaven
    Coveted her and me.

And this was the reason that, long ago,
    In this kingdom by the sea,
A wind blew out of a cloud by night
    Chilling my Annabel Lee;
So that her high-born kinsmen came
    And bore her away from me,
To shut her up in a sepulchre
    In this kingdom by the sea.

The angels, not half so happy in Heaven,
    Went envying her and me;
Yes! that was the reason (as all men know,
    In this kingdom by the sea)
That the wind came out of the cloud, chilling
    And killing my Annabel Lee.

But our love it was stronger by far than the love
    Of those who were older than we —
    Of many far wiser than we —
And neither the angels in Heaven above
    Nor the demons down under the sea
Can ever dissever my soul from the soul
    Of the beautiful Annabel Lee: —

For the moon never beams without bringing me dreams
    Of the beautiful Annabel Lee;
And the stars never rise but I see the bright eyes
    Of the beautiful Annabel Lee;
And so, all the night-tide, I lie down by the side
Of my darling, my darling, my life and my bride
    In her sepulchre there by the sea —
    In her tomb by the side of the sea.

OLIVER WENDELL HOLMES, SR. *(1809–1894)*

A prominent Harvard physician (and father of the distinguished jurist of the same name), Holmes wrote "Old Ironsides" at age 21 in a successful effort to prevent destruction of the celebrated warship *Constitution*, which may still be viewed today.

Old Ironsides

Ay, tear her tattered ensign down!
    Long has it waved on high,
And many an eye has danced to see
    That banner in the sky;
Beneath it rung the battle shout,
    And burst the cannon's roar; —
The meteor of the ocean air
    Shall sweep the clouds no more!

Her deck, once red with heroes' blood
    Where knelt the vanquished foe,
When winds were hurrying o'er the flood
    And waves were white below,
No more shall feel the victor's tread,
    Or know the conquered knee; —
The harpies of the shore shall pluck
    The eagle of the sea!

O better that her shattered hulk
    Should sink beneath the wave;
Her thunders shook the mighty deep,
    And there should be her grave;
Nail to the mast her holy flag,
    Set every thread-bare sail,
And give her to the god of storms, —
    The lightning and the gale!

The Chambered Nautilus

This is the ship of pearl, which, poets feign,
    Sails the unshadowed main, —
    The venturous bark that flings

On the sweet summer wind its purpled wings
In gulfs enchanted, where the siren sings,
　　And coral reefs lie bare,
Where the cold sea-maids rise to sun their streaming hair.

Its webs of living gauze no more unfurl;
　　Wrecked is the ship of pearl!
　　And every chambered cell,
Where its dim dreaming life was wont to dwell,
As the frail tenant shaped his growing shell,
　　Before thee lies revealed, —
Its irised ceiling rent, its sunless crypt unsealed!

Year after year beheld the silent toil
　　That spread his lustrous coil;
　　Still, as the spiral grew,
He left the past year's dwelling for the new,
Stole with soft step its shining archway through,
　　Built up its idle door,
Stretched in his last-found home, and knew the old no more.

Thanks for the heavenly message brought by thee,
　　Child of the wandering sea,
　　Cast from her lap forlorn!
From thy dead lips a clearer note is born
Than ever Triton blew from wreathèd horn!
　　While on mine ear it rings,
Through the deep caves of thought I hear a voice that sings: —

Build thee more stately mansions, O my soul,
　　As the swift seasons roll!
　　Leave thy low-vaulted past!
Let each new temple, nobler than the last,
Shut thee from heaven with a dome more vast,
　　Till thou at length art free,
Leaving thine outgrown shell by life's unresting sea!

ALFRED, LORD TENNYSON *(1809–1892)*

Tennyson was the most famous and respected English poet of the Victorian era. Poet Laureate from 1850 until his death, he served as the literary voice of an empire. "The Charge of the Light Brigade" was inspired by a tragic battle during the Crimean War.

The Charge of the Light Brigade

I   Half a league, half a league,
Half a league onward,
All in the valley of Death
    Rode the six hundred.
"Forward the Light Brigade!
Charge for the guns!" he said.
Into the valley of Death
    Rode the six hundred.

II   "Forward, the Light Brigade!"
Was there a man dismay'd?
Not tho' the soldier knew
   Some one had blunder'd.
Theirs not to make reply,
Theirs not to reason why,
Theirs but to do and die.
Into the valley of Death
    Rode the six hundred.

III   Cannon to right of them,
Cannon to left of them,
Cannon in front of them
    Volley'd and thunder'd;
Storm'd at with shot and shell,
Boldly they rode and well,
Into the jaws of Death,
Into the mouth of hell
    Rode the six hundred.

IV   Flash'd all their sabres bare,
Flash'd as they turn'd in air
Sabring the gunners there,
Charging an army, while
    All the world wonder'd.

Plunged in the battery-smoke
Right thro' the line they broke;
Cossack and Russian
Reel'd from the sabre-stroke
   Shatter'd and sunder'd.
Then they rode back, but not,
   Not the six hundred.

v .Cannon to right of them,
Cannon to left of them,
Cannon behind them
   Volley'd and thunder'd;
Storm'd at with shot and shell,
While horse and hero fell,
They that had fought so well
Came thro' the jaws of Death,
Back from the mouth of hell,
All that was left of them,
   Left of six hundred.

vi   When can their glory fade?
O the wild charge they made!
   All the world wonder'd.
Honour the charge they made!
Honour the Light Brigade,
   Noble six hundred!

Crossing the Bar

Sunset and evening star,
   And one clear call for me!
And may there be no moaning of the bar,
   When I put out to sea,

But such a tide as moving seems asleep,
   Too full for sound and foam,
When that which drew from out the boundless deep
   Turns again home.

Twilight and evening bell,
   And after that the dark!
And may there be no sadness of farewell,
   When I embark;

For tho' from out our bourne of Time and Place
   The flood may bear me far,
I hope to see my Pilot face to face
   When I have crost the bar.

ROBERT BROWNING *(1812–1889)*

Although he stands with Tennyson as one of the seminal Victorian poets, Browning enjoyed little of his counterpart's public success until late in his life. He is today best remembered for perfectly wrought dramatic monologues such as "My Last Duchess."

My Last Duchess

FERRARA

That's my last Duchess painted on the wall,
Looking as if she were alive. I call
That piece a wonder, now: Frà Pandolf's hands
Worked busily a day, and there she stands.
Will 't please you sit and look at her? I said
"Frà Pandolf" by design: for never read
Strangers like you that pictured countenance,
The depth and passion of its earnest glance,
But to myself they turned (since none puts by
The curtain I have drawn for you, but I)
And seemed as they would ask me, if they durst,
How such a glance came there; so, not the first
Are you to turn and ask thus. Sir, 't was not
Her husband's presence only, called that spot
Of joy into the Duchess' cheek: perhaps
Frà Pandolf chanced to say "Her mantle laps
Over my lady's wrist too much," or "Paint
Must never hope to reproduce the faint
Half-flush that dies along her throat:" such stuff
Was courtesy, she thought, and cause enough
For calling up that spot of joy. She had
A heart—how shall I say?—too soon made glad,
Too easily impressed; she liked whate'er
She looked on, and her looks went everywhere.
Sir, 't was all one! My favour at her breast,
The dropping of the daylight in the West,
The bough of cherries some officious fool

Broke in the orchard for her, the white mule
She rode with round the terrace — all and each
Would draw from her alike the approving speech,
Or blush, at least. She thanked men, — good! but thanked
Somehow — I know not how — as if she ranked
My gift of a nine-hundred-years-old name
With anybody's gift. Who'd stoop to blame
This sort of trifling? Even had you skill
In speech — (which I have not) — to make your will
Quite clear to such an one, and say, "Just this
Or that in you disgusts me; here you miss,
Or there exceed the mark" — and if she let
Herself be lessoned so, nor plainly set
Her wits to yours, forsooth, and made excuse,
— E'en then would be some stooping; and I choose
Never to stoop. Oh sir, she smiled, no doubt,
Whene'er I passed her; but who passed without
Much the same smile? This grew; I gave commands;
Then all smiles stopped together. There she stands
As if alive. Will 't please you rise? We'll meet
The company below, then. I repeat,
The Count your master's known munificence
Is ample warrant that no just pretence
Of mine for dowry will be disallowed;
Though his fair daughter's self, as I avowed
At starting, is my object. Nay, we'll go
Together down, sir. Notice Neptune, though,
Taming a sea-horse, thought a rarity,
Which Claus of Innsbruck cast in bronze for me!

WALT WHITMAN *(1819–1892)*

Whitman was the conscious author of avowedly American writings, and established an expansive style that is one of the most distinctive in the nation's literature. "O Captain! My Captain!" was written shortly after the death of Abraham Lincoln.

I Hear America Singing

I hear America singing, the varied carols I hear,
Those of mechanics, each one singing his as it should be blithe and
    strong,
The carpenter singing his as he measures his plank or beam,

The mason singing his as he makes ready for work, or leaves off
    work,
The boatman singing what belongs to him in his boat, the deck-
    hand singing on the steamboat deck,
The shoemaker singing as he sits on his bench, the hatter singing as
    he stands,
The wood-cutter's song, the ploughboy's on his way in the morn-
    ing, or at noon intermission or at sundown,
The delicious singing of the mother, or of the young wife at work,
    or of the girl sewing or washing,
Each singing what belongs to him or her and to none else,
The day what belongs to the day—at night the party of young
    fellows, robust, friendly,
Singing with open mouths their strong melodious songs.

O Captain! My Captain!

1

O captain! my captain! our fearful trip is done;
The ship has weather'd every rack, the prize we sought is won;
The port is near, the bells I hear, the people all exulting,
While follow eyes the steady keel, the vessel grim and daring:
        But O heart! heart! heart!
           Leave you not the little spot,
              Where on the deck my captain lies,
                Fallen cold and dead.

2

O captain! my captain! rise up and hear the bells;
Rise up—for you the flag is flung—for you the bugle trills;
For you bouquets and ribbon'd wreaths—for you the shores
    a-crowding;
For you they call, the swaying mass, their eager faces turning;
        O captain! dear father!
           This arm I push beneath you;
              It is some dream that on the deck,
                You've fallen cold and dead.

3

My captain does not answer, his lips are pale and still;
My father does not feel my arm, he has no pulse nor will:

But the ship, the ship is anchor'd safe, its voyage closed and done;
From fearful trip, the victor ship, comes in with object won:
    Exult, O shores, and ring, O bells!
      But I, with silent tread,
        Walk the spot my captain lies,
          Fallen cold and dead.

A Noiseless Patient Spider

A noiseless patient spider,
I mark'd where on a little promontory it stood isolated,
Mark'd how to explore the vacant vast surrounding,
It launch'd forth filament, filament, filament, out of itself,
Ever unreeling them, ever tirelessly speeding them.

And you O my soul where you stand,
Surrounded, detached, in measureless oceans of space,
Ceaselessly musing, venturing, throwing, seeking the spheres to
    connect them,
Till the bridge you will need be form'd, till the ductile anchor hold,
Till the gossamer thread you fling catch somewhere, O my soul.

MATTHEW ARNOLD *(1822–1888)*

One of the most influential critics of the mid-Victorian Age, Arnold also created important poetic works. The most famous of these, "Dover Beach," has come to be seen as one of the seminal expressions of the spirit of Arnold's time.

Dover Beach

The sea is calm to-night,
The tide is full, the moon lies fair
Upon the Straits; — on the French coast, the light
Gleams, and is gone; the cliffs of England stand,
Glimmering and vast, out in the tranquil bay.
Come to the window, sweet is the night air!
Only, from the long line of spray
Where the ebb meets the moon-blanch'd sand,
Listen! you hear the grating roar
Of pebbles which the waves suck back, and fling,
At their return, up the high strand,

Begin, and cease, and then again begin,
With tremulous cadence slow, and bring
The eternal note of sadness in.

Sophocles long ago
Heard it on the Aegaean, and it brought
Into his mind the turbid ebb and flow
Of human misery; we
Find also in the sound a thought,
Hearing it by this distant northern sea.

The sea of faith
Was once, too, at the full, and round earth's shore
Lay like the folds of a bright girdle furl'd;
But now I only hear
Its melancholy, long, withdrawing roar,
Retreating to the breath
Of the night-wind down the vast edges drear
And naked shingles of the world.

Ah, love, let us be true
To one another! for the world, which seems
To lie before us like a land of dreams,
So various, so beautiful, so new,
Hath really neither joy, nor love, nor light,
Nor certitude, nor peace, nor help for pain;
And we are here as on a darkling plain
Swept with confused alarms of struggle and flight,
Where ignorant armies clash by night.

GEORGE MEREDITH *(1828–1909)*

Remembered principally as a novelist, Meredith was by preference a poet (he wrote with distinction in both forms). His verses combine an energetic flair for drama with an often sardonic pessimism.

Lucifer in Starlight

On a starred night Prince Lucifer uprose.
    Tired of his dark dominion, swung the fiend
    Above the rolling ball in cloud part screened,
Where sinners hugged their spectre of repose.

Poor prey to his hot fit of pride were those.
   And now upon his western wing he leaned,
   Now his huge bulk o'er Afric's sands careened,
Now the black planet shadowed Arctic snows.
Soaring through wider zones that pricked his scars
   With memory of the old revolt from Awe,
He reached a middle height, and at the stars,
Which are the brain of heaven, he looked, and sank.
Around the ancient track marched, rank on rank,
   The army of unalterable law.

EMILY DICKINSON *(1830–1886)*

One of the giants of American literature, Dickinson lived her life as a near-recluse, writing her poems on scraps of paper. Collected and published after her death, they have come to be regarded as among the most brilliant and original verses in the language.

"I'm Nobody! Who Are You?"

I'm nobody! Who are you?
Are you nobody, too?
Then there's a pair of us — don't tell!
They'd banish us, you know.

How dreary to be somebody!
How public, like a frog
To tell your name the livelong day
To an admiring bog!

"This Is My Letter to the World"

This is my letter to the world,
   That never wrote to me, —
The simple news that Nature told,
   With tender majesty.

Her message is committed
   To hands I cannot see;
For love of her, sweet countrymen,
   Judge tenderly of me!

"I Heard a Fly Buzz When I Died"

I heard a fly buzz when I died;
    The stillness round my form
Was like the stillness in the air
    Between the heaves of storm.

The eyes beside had wrung them dry,
    And breaths were gathering sure
For that last onset, when the king
    Be witnessed in his power.

I willed my keepsakes, signed away
    What portion of me I
Could make assignable, — and then
    There interposed a fly,

With blue, uncertain, stumbling buzz,
    Between the light and me;
And then the windows failed, and then
    I could not see to see.

"Because I Could Not Stop for Death"

Because I could not stop for Death,
He kindly stopped for me;
The carriage held but just ourselves
And Immortality.

We slowly drove, he knew no haste,
And I had put away
My labor, and my leisure too,
For his civility.

We passed the school where children played,
Their lessons scarcely done;
We passed the fields of gazing grain,
We passed the setting sun.

We paused before a house that seemed
A swelling of the ground;
The roof was scarcely visible,
The cornice but a mound.

Since then 't is centuries; but each
Feels shorter than the day
I first surmised the horses' heads
Were toward eternity.

CHRISTINA ROSSETTI *(1830–1894)*

Sister of Pre-Raphaelite painter and poet Dante Gabriel Rossetti, Christina Rossetti wrote verses that combined the sensuality of her aesthetic heritage with a fervent commitment to the Anglican faith.

A Birthday

My heart is like a singing bird
   Whose nest is in a water'd shoot;
My heart is like an apple-tree
   Whose boughs are bent with thick-set fruit;
My heart is like a rainbow shell
   That paddles in a halcyon sea;
My heart is gladder than all these,
   Because my love is come to me.

Raise me a daïs of silk and down;
   Hang it with vair and purple dyes;
Carve it in doves and pomegranates,
   And peacocks with a hundred eyes;
Work it in gold and silver grapes,
   In leaves and silver fleurs-de-lys;
Because the birthday of my life
   Is come, my love is come to me.

LEWIS CARROLL *(1832–1898)*

Immortalized as the author of *Alice's Adventures in Wonderland,* "Lewis Carroll" was the pseudonym of Oxford mathematician Charles Lutwidge Dodgson. "Jabberwocky," probably the most celebrated nonsense poem in English, first appeared in *Alice's* sequel, *Through the Looking-Glass and What Alice Found There* (1871).

Jabberwocky

'Twas brillig, and the slithy toves
   Did gyre and gimble in the wabe:
All mimsy were the borogoves,
   And the mome raths outgrabe.

"Beware the Jabberwock, my son!
   The jaws that bite, the claws that catch!

Beware the Jubjub bird, and shun
   The frumious Bandersnatch!"

He took his vorpal sword in hand:
   Long time the manxome foe he sought—
So rested he by the Tumtum tree,
   And stood awhile in thought.

And, as in uffish thought he stood,
   The Jabberwock, with eyes of flame,
Came whiffling through the tulgey wood,
   And burbled as it came!

One, two! One, two! And through and through
   The vorpal blade went snicker-snack!
He left it dead, and with its head
   He went galumphing back.

"And hast thou slain the Jabberwock?
   Come to my arms, my beamish boy!
O frabjous day! Callooh! Callay!"
   He chortled in his joy.

'Twas brillig, and the slithy toves
   Did gyre and gimble in the wabe:
All mimsy were the borogoves,
   And the mome raths outgrabe.

THOMAS HARDY *(1840–1928)*

Having established a place for himself among the greatest English novelists, Hardy
turned to poetry late in his career; nonetheless, his verses achieved a rare distinction
and have exerted a wide influence.

The Darkling Thrush

I leant upon a coppice gate
   When Frost was spectre-gray,
And Winter's dregs made desolate
   The weakening eye of day.
The tangled bine-stems scored the sky
   Like strings from broken lyres,
And all mankind that haunted nigh
   Had sought their household fires.

The land's sharp features seemed to be
    The Century's corpse outleant,
His crypt the cloudy canopy,
    The wind his death-lament.
The ancient pulse of germ and birth
    Was shrunken hard and dry,
And every spirit upon earth
    Seemed fervourless as I.

At once a voice arose among
    The bleak twigs overhead
In a full-hearted evensong
    Of joy illimited;
An aged thrush, frail, gaunt, and small,
    In blast-beruffled plume,
Had chosen thus to fling his soul
    Upon the growing gloom.

So little cause for carollings
    Of such ecstatic sound
Was written on terrestrial things
    Afar or nigh around,
That I could think there trembled through
    His happy good-night air
Some blessed Hope, whereof he knew
    And I was unaware.

GERARD MANLEY HOPKINS *(1844–1889)*

A Jesuit priest, Hopkins never published during his lifetime. His idiosyncratic poems exhibit technical and linguistic innovations that still seem daring, and reflect their author's passionate spiritual life.

The Windhover:

TO CHRIST OUR LORD

I caught this morning morning's minion, king-
    dom of daylight's dauphin, dapple-dawn-drawn Falcon, in his
        riding
    Of the rolling level underneath him steady air, and striding
High there, how he rung upon the rein of a wimpling wing

In his ecstasy! then off, off forth on swing,
    As a skate's heel sweeps smooth on a bow-bend: the hurl and
        gliding
    Rebuffed the big wind. My heart in hiding
Stirred for a bird, — the achieve of, the mastery of the thing!

Brute beauty and valour and act, oh, air, pride, plume, here
    Buckle! AND the fire that breaks from thee then, a billion
Times told lovelier, more dangerous, O my chevalier!

    No wonder of it: shéer plód makes plough down sillion
Shine, and blue-bleak embers, ah my dear,
    Fall, gall themselves, and gash gold-vermilion.

Pied Beauty

Glory be to God for dappled things—
    For skies of couple-colour as a brinded cow;
        For rose-moles all in stipple upon trout that swim;
Fresh-firecoal chestnut-falls; finches' wings;
    Landscape plotted and pieced—fold, fallow, and plough;
        And áll trádes, their gear and tackle and trim.

All things counter, original, spare, strange;
    Whatever is fickle, freckled (who knows how?)
        With swift, slow; sweet, sour; adazzle, dim;
He fathers-forth whose beauty is past change:
                    Praise him.

ROBERT LOUIS STEVENSON *(1850–1894)*

The author of *Treasure Island* and other widely read works, Stevenson spent most of his life traveling the world in an effort to overcome his chronic tuberculosis. "Requiem" is carved onto the poet's gravestone, in Samoa.

Requiem

Under the wide and starry sky
Dig the grave and let me lie;
Glad did I live and gladly die,
And I laid me down with a will.

This be the verse you grave for me:
Here he lies where he longed to be;
Home is the sailor, home from sea,
And the hunter home from the hill.

A. E. HOUSMAN *(1859–1936)*

Housman was a noted British Latin scholar whose poems combined simplicity and craft in a manner that found favor with both critics and the reading public. "To an Athlete Dying Young" is from his celebrated collection A *Shropshire Lad* (1896).

To an Athlete Dying Young

The time you won your town the race
We chaired you through the market-place;
Man and boy stood cheering by,
And home we brought you shoulder-high.

To-day, the road all runners come,
Shoulder-high we bring you home,
And set you at your threshold down,
Townsman of a stiller town.

Smart lad, to slip betimes away
From fields where glory does not stay
And early though the laurel grows
It withers quicker than the rose.

Eyes the shady night has shut
Cannot see the record cut,
And silence sounds no worse than cheers
After earth has stopped the ears:

Now you will not swell the rout
Of lads that wore their honours out,
Runners whom renown outran
And the name died before the man.

So set, before its echoes fade,
The fleet foot on the sill of shade,
And hold to the low lintel up
The still-defended challenge-cup.

And round that early-laurelled head
Will flock to gaze the strengthless dead,
And find unwithered on its curls
The garland briefer than a girl's.

RUDYARD KIPLING *(1865–1936)*

An author who achieved distinction and enormous popularity with his fiction and verses, Kipling remains the essential voice of late-Victorian colonialism. Despite radical shifts in public taste since that era, his writings continue to attract readers by their sheer excellence.

Gunga Din

You may talk o' gin and beer
When you're quartered safe out 'ere,
An' you're sent to penny-fights an' Aldershot[1] it;
But when it comes to slaughter
You will do your work on water,
An' you'll lick the bloomin' boots of 'im that's got it.
Now in Injia's sunny clime,
Where I used to spend my time
A-servin' of 'Er Majesty the Queen,
Of all them blackfaced crew
The finest man I knew
Was our regimental bhisti,[2] Gunga Din.
      He was "Din! Din! Din!
      You limping lump o' brick-dust, Gunga Din!
      Hi! slippery hitherao!
      Water, get it! Panee lao![3]
      You squidgy-nosed old idol, Gunga Din."

The uniform 'e wore
Was nothin' much before,
An' rather less than 'arf o' that be'ind,
For a piece o' twisty rag
An' a goatskin water-bag

---

[1] *Aldershot*] military camp near London.
[2] *bhisti*] water carrier.
[3] *Panee lao*] Bring water swiftly.

Was all the field-equipment 'e could find.
When the sweatin' troop-train lay
In a sidin' through the day,
Where the 'eat would make your bloomin' eyebrows crawl,
We shouted "Harry By!"[4]
Till our throats were bricky-dry,
Then we wopped 'im 'cause 'e couldn't serve us all.
     It was "Din! Din! Din!
     You 'eathen, where the mischief 'ave you been?
     You put some juldee[5] in it
     Or I'll marrow[6] you this minute
     If you don't fill up my helmet, Gunga Din!"

'E would dot an' carry one
     Till the longest day was done;
An' 'e didn't seem to know the use o' fear.
     If we charged or broke or cut,
     You could bet your bloomin' nut,
'E'd be waitin' fifty paces right flank rear.
     With 'is mussick[7] on 'is back,
     'E would skip with our attack,
An' watch us till the bugles made "Retire,"
     An' for all 'is dirty 'ide
     'E was white, clear white, inside
When 'e went to tend the wounded under fire!
     It was "Din! Din! Din!"
With the bullets kickin' dust-spots on the green.
     When the cartridges ran out,
     You could hear the front-files shout,
"Hi! ammunition-mules an' Gunga Din!"

I sha'n't forgit the night
     When I dropped be'ind the fight
With a bullet where my belt-plate should 'a' been.
     I was chokin' mad with thirst,
     An' the man that spied me first
Was our good old grinnin', gruntin' Gunga Din.
     'E lifted up my 'ead,

---

[4] *Harry By*] enlisted man's equivalent for "O brother."
[5] *juldee*] be quick.
[6] *marrow*] hit.
[7] *mussick*] water skin.

An' he plugged me where I bled,
An' 'e guv me 'arf-a-pint o' water-green:
It was crawlin' and it stunk,
But of all the drinks I've drunk,
I'm gratefullest to one from Gunga Din.
It was "Din! Din! Din!"
'Ere's a beggar with a bullet through 'is spleen;
'E's chawin' up the ground,
An' 'e's kickin' all around:
For Gawd's sake git the water, Gunga Din!

'E carried me away
To where a dooli[8] lay,
An' a bullet come an' drilled the beggar clean.
'E put me safe inside,
An' just before 'e died:
"I 'ope you liked your drink," sez Gunga Din.
So I'll meet 'im later on
At the place where 'e is gone —
Where it's always double drill and no canteen;
'E'll be squattin' on the coals,
Givin' drink to poor damned souls,
An' I'll get a swig in hell from Gunga Din!
Yes, Din! Din! Din!
You Lazarushian-leather[9] Gunga Din!
Though I've belted you and flayed you,
By the living Gawd that made you,
You're a better man than I am, Gunga Din!

Recessional

(A VICTORIAN ODE)

God of our fathers, known of old —
    Lord of our far-flung battle line —
Beneath whose awful hand we hold
    Dominion over palm and pine —
Lord God of Hosts, be with us yet,
Lest we forget — lest we forget!

---

[8] *dooli*] stretcher.
[9] *Lazarushian-leather*] humorous combination of "Lazarus" and "Russian leather."

The tumult and the shouting dies —
  The Captains and the Kings depart —
Still stands Thine ancient sacrifice,
  An humble and a contrite heart.
Lord God of Hosts, be with us yet,
Lest we forget — lest we forget!

Far-called our navies melt away —
  On dune and headland sinks the fire —
Lo, all our pomp of yesterday
  Is one with Nineveh and Tyre!
Judge of the Nations, spare us yet,
Lest we forget — lest we forget!

If, drunk with sight of power, we loose
  Wild tongues that have not Thee in awe —
Such boastings as the Gentiles use,
  Or lesser breeds without the Law —
Lord God of Hosts, be with us yet,
Lest we forget — lest we forget!

For heathen heart that puts her trust
  In reeking tube and iron shard —
All valiant dust that builds on dust,
  And guarding calls not Thee to guard.
For frantic boast and foolish word,
Thy Mercy on Thy People, Lord!
                                    Amen.

If —

If you can keep your head when all about you
  Are losing theirs and blaming it on you,
If you can trust yourself when all men doubt you,
  But make allowance for their doubting too;
If you can wait and not be tired by waiting,
  Or being lied about, don't deal in lies,
Or being hated don't give way to hating,
  And yet don't look too good, nor talk too wise:

If you can dream — and not make dreams your master;
  If you can think — and not make thoughts your aim,
If you can meet with Triumph and Disaster
  And treat those two impostors just the same;

If you can bear to hear the truth you've spoken
    Twisted by knaves to make a trap for fools,
Or watch the things you gave your life to, broken,
    And stoop and build 'em up with worn-out tools:

If you can make one heap of all your winnings
    And risk it on one turn of pitch-and-toss,
And lose, and start again at your beginnings
    And never breathe a word about your loss;
If you can force your heart and nerve and sinew
    To serve your turn long after they are gone,
And so hold on when there is nothing in you
    Except the Will which says to them: "Hold on!"

If you can talk with crowds and keep your virtue,
    Or walk with Kings — nor lose the common touch,
If neither foes nor loving friends can hurt you,
    If all men count with you, but none too much;
If you can fill the unforgiving minute
    With sixty seconds' worth of distance run,
Yours is the Earth and everything that's in it,
    And — which is more — you'll be a Man, my son!

WILLIAM BUTLER YEATS *(1865–1939)*

Perhaps the most distinguished poet of the early twentieth century, Yeats fused elements of his Irish heritage with a modern temperament to create a matchless body of moving, well-wrought verse.

The Lake Isle of Innisfree

I will arise and go now, and go to Innisfree,
And a small cabin build there, of clay and wattles made:
Nine bean rows will I have there, a hive for the honey bee,
And live alone in the bee-loud glade.

And I shall have some peace there, for peace comes dropping slow,
Dropping from the veils of the morning to where the cricket sings;
There midnight's all a glimmer, and noon a purple glow,
And evening full of the linnet's wings.

I wiil arise and go now, for always night and day
I hear lake water lapping with low sounds by the shore;
While I stand on the roadway, or on the pavements gray,
I hear it in the deep heart's core.

When You Are Old

When you are old and gray and full of sleep,
And nodding by the fire, take down this book,
And slowly read, and dream of the soft look
Your eyes had once, and of their shadows deep;

How many loved your moments of glad grace,
And loved your beauty with love false or true;
But one man loved the pilgrim soul in you,
And loved the sorrows of your changing face.

And bending down beside the glowing bars
Murmur, a little sadly, how love fled
And paced upon the mountains overhead
And hid his face amid a crowd of stars.

The Second Coming

Turning and turning in the widening gyre
The falcon cannot hear the falconer;
Things fall apart; the centre cannot hold;
Mere anarchy is loosed upon the world,
The blood-dimmed tide is loosed, and everywhere
The ceremony of innocence is drowned;
The best lack all conviction, while the worst
Are full of passionate intensity.

Surely some revelation is at hand;
Surely the Second Coming is at hand.
The Second Coming! Hardly are those words out
When a vast image out of *Spiritus Mundi*[1]
Troubles my sight: somewhere in sands of the desert
A shape with lion body and the head of a man,
A gaze blank and pitiless as the sun,

---

[1] *Spiritus Mundi*] The "universal soul," or collective unconscious.

Is moving its slow thighs, while all about it
Reel shadows of the indignant desert birds.
The darkness drops again; but now I know
That twenty centuries of stony sleep
Were vexed to nightmare by a rocking cradle,
And what rough beast, its hour come round at last,
Slouches towards Bethlehem to be born?

EDWIN ARLINGTON ROBINSON *(1869–1935)*

Robinson's literary career was slow in starting, but he ultimately established himself as one of America's most honored poets, winning three Pulitzer prizes and popularizing an honest and forthright style.

Richard Cory

Whenever Richard Cory went down town,
We people on the pavement looked at him:
He was a gentleman from sole to crown,
Clean favored, and imperially slim.

And he was always quietly arrayed,
And he was always human when he talked;
But still he fluttered pulses when he said,
"Good-morning," and he glittered when he walked.

And he was rich — yes, richer than a king —
And admirably schooled in every grace:
In fine, we thought that he was everything
To make us wish that we were in his place.

So on we worked, and waited for the light,
And went without the meat, and cursed the bread;
And Richard Cory, one calm summer night,
Went home and put a bullet through his head.

Miniver Cheevy

Miniver Cheevy, child of scorn,
    Grew lean while he assailed the seasons;
He wept that he was ever born,
    And he had reasons.

Miniver loved the days of old
  When swords were bright and steeds were prancing;
The vision of a warrior bold
  Would set him dancing.

Miniver sighed for what was not,
  And dreamed, and rested from his labors;
He dreamed of Thebes and Camelot,
  And Priam's neighbors.

Miniver mourned the ripe renown
  That made so many a name so fragrant;
He mourned Romance, now on the town,
  And Art, a vagrant.

Miniver loved the Medici,
  Albeit he had never seen one;
He would have sinned incessantly
  Could he have been one.

Miniver cursed the commonplace
  And eyed a khaki suit with loathing;
He missed the mediæval grace
  Of iron clothing.

Miniver scorned the gold he sought,
  But sore annoyed was he without it;
Miniver thought, and thought, and thought,
  And thought about it.

Miniver Cheevy, born too late,
  Scratched his head and kept on thinking;
Miniver coughed, and called it fate,
  And kept on drinking.

ROBERT FROST *(1874–1963)*

One of America's most popular poets, Frost also commands a great deal of critical respect for his finely rendered works, which combine clear and memorable language with a frequently dark, modern sensibility.

The Road Not Taken

Two roads diverged in a yellow wood,
And sorry I could not travel both
And be one traveler, long I stood
And looked down one as far as I could
To where it bent in the undergrowth;

Then took the other, as just as fair,
And having perhaps the better claim,
Because it was grassy and wanted wear;
Though as for that the passing there
Had worn them really about the same,

And both that morning equally lay
In leaves no step had trodden black.
Oh, I kept the first for another day!
Yet knowing how way leads on to way,
I doubted if I should ever come back.

I shall be telling this with a sigh
Somewhere ages and ages hence:
Two roads diverged in a wood, and I—
I took the one less traveled by,
And that has made all the difference.

Stopping by Woods on a Snowy Evening

Whose woods these are I think I know.
His house is in the village though;
He will not see me stopping here
To watch his woods fill up with snow.

My little horse must think it queer
To stop without a farmhouse near
Between the woods and frozen lake
The darkest evening of the year.

He gives his harness bells a shake
To ask if there is some mistake.
The only other sound's the sweep
Of easy wind and downy flake.

The woods are lovely, dark and deep.
But I have promises to keep,
And miles to go before I sleep,
And miles to go before I sleep.

CARL SANDBURG *(1878–1967)*

An Illinois native whose early life was spent working a variety of menial jobs, Sandburg rose to prominence in the 1910s as a poetic voice of the common folk and the most popular writer of the "Chicago Renaissance."

Chicago

> Hog Butcher for the World,
> Tool Maker, Stacker of Wheat,
> Player with Railroads and the Nation's Freight Handler;
> Stormy, husky, brawling,
> City of the Big Shoulders:

They tell me you are wicked and I believe them, for I have seen your painted women under the gas lamps luring the farm boys.
And they tell me you are crooked and I answer: Yes, it is true I have seen the gunman kill and go free to kill again.
And they tell me you are brutal and my reply is: On the faces of women and children I have seen the marks of wanton hunger.
And having answered so I turn once more to those who sneer at this my city, and I give them back the sneer and say to them:
Come and show me another city with lifted head singing so proud to be alive and coarse and strong and cunning.
Flinging magnetic curses amid the toil of piling job on job, here is a tall bold slugger set vivid against the little soft cities;
Fierce as a dog with tongue lapping for action, cunning as a savage pitted against the wilderness,
> Bareheaded,
> Shoveling,
> Wrecking,

          Planning,
          Building, breaking, rebuilding,
Under the smoke, dust all over his mouth, laughing with white
      teeth,
Under the terrible burden of destiny laughing as a young man
      laughs,
Laughing even as an ignorant fighter laughs who has never lost a
      battle,
Bragging and laughing that under his wrist is the pulse, and under
      his ribs the heart of the people,
                  Laughing!
Laughing the stormy, husky, brawling laughter of Youth, half-
      naked, sweating, proud to be Hog Butcher, Tool Maker,
      Stacker of Wheat, Player with Railroads and Freight Handler
      to the Nation.

Fog

The fog comes
on little cat feet.

It sits looking
over harbor and city
on silent haunches
and then moves on.

WALLACE STEVENS *(1879–1955)*

An insurance executive who wrote some of the most accomplished and demanding
poetry in American literature during his spare moments, Stevens combines flawless
craftsmanship and linguistic sheen with sharp existential considerations.

The Emperor of Ice-Cream

Call the roller of big cigars,
The muscular one, and bid him whip
In kitchen cups concupiscent curds.
Let the wenches dawdle in such dress
As they are used to wear, and let the boys
Bring flowers in last month's newspapers.
Let be be finale of seem.
The only emperor is the emperor of ice-cream.

Take from the dresser of deal,
Lacking the three glass knobs, that sheet
On which she embroidered fantails once
And spread it so as to cover her face.
If her horny feet protrude, they come
To show how cold she is, and dumb.
Let the lamp affix its beam.
The only emperor is the emperor of ice-cream.

WILLIAM CARLOS WILLIAMS *(1883–1963)*

Williams combined an active practice as a New Jersey physician with a literary career that lasted over half a century. A pioneer modernist, Williams is known for his use of mundane physical imagery, as in "The Red Wheelbarrow."

The Red Wheelbarrow

so much depends
upon

a red wheel
barrow

glazed with rain
water

beside the white
chickens

EZRA POUND *(1885–1972)*

For decades Pound lived an expatriate's life in Europe, exerting a strong influence on many important modernist writers. His lifelong interest in Asian aesthetics and literature is manifest in this early (and free) translation.

The River-Merchant's Wife: A Letter

TRANSLATED FROM THE CHINESE OF LI PO [RIHAKU]

While my hair was still cut straight across my forehead
I played about the front gate, pulling flowers.
You came by on bamboo stilts, playing horse,

You walked about my seat, playing with blue plums.
And we went on living in the village of Chokan:
Two small people, without dislike or suspicion.

At fourteen I married My Lord you.
I never laughed, being bashful.
Lowering my head, I looked at the wall.
Called to, a thousand times, I never looked back.

At fifteen I stopped scowling,
I desired my dust to be mingled with yours
Forever and forever and forever.
Why should I climb the look out?

At sixteen you departed,
You went into far Ku-to-yen, by the river of swirling eddies,
And you have been gone five months.
The monkeys make sorrowful noise overhead.
You dragged your feet when you went out.
By the gate now, the moss is grown, the different mosses,
Too deep to clear them away!
The leaves fall early this autumn, in wind.
The paired butterflies are already yellow with August
Over the grass in the West garden;
They hurt me. I grow older.
If you are coming down through the narrows of the river Kiang,
Please let me know beforehand,
And I will come out to meet you
                    As far as Cho-fu-sa.

MARIANNE MOORE *(1887–1972)*

A highly personal yet uncompromising poet, Moore wrote disciplined, frequently
ironic poems reflective of her wide-ranging intellect and strength of spirit. Moore
was also a prominent literary editor and critic.

Poetry

I, too, dislike it: there are things that are important beyond all
    this fiddle.
    Reading it, however, with a perfect contempt for it, one
        discovers in

it after all, a place for the genuine.
  Hands that can grasp, eyes
  that can dilate, hair that can rise
    if it must, these things are important not because a

high-sounding interpretation can be put upon them but because
    they are
  useful. When they become so derivative as to become
    unintelligible,
  the same thing may be said for all of us, that we
  do not admire what
  we cannot understand: the bat
    holding on upside down or in quest of something to

eat, elephants pushing, a wild horse taking a roll, a tireless wolf
    under
  a tree, the immovable critic twitching his skin like a horse that
    feels a
  flea, the base-
  ball fan, the statistician —
  nor is it valid
    to discriminate against 'business documents and

school-books'; all these phenomena are important. One must
    make a distinction
  however: when dragged into prominence by half poets, the
    result is not poetry,
  nor till the poets among us can be
    'literalists of
    the imagination' — above
      insolence and triviality and can present

for inspection, 'imaginary gardens with real toads in them', shall
    we have
  it. In the meantime, if you demand on the one hand,
  the raw material of poetry in
    all its rawness and
    that which is on the other hand
      genuine, you are interested in poetry.

EDNA ST. VINCENT MILLAY *(1892–1950)*

A poet frequently associated with the bohemian life of Greenwich Village, Millay was a visible presence on the literary scene of the 1910s and 20s. "First Fig" memorably summarizes her public persona.

First Fig

My candle burns at both ends;
    It will not last the night;
But ah, my foes and oh, my friends —
    It gives a lovely light.

WILFRED OWEN *(1893–1918)*

Owen was killed as an English soldier at age 25, one week before the armistice that ended World War I. His poems, most of which deal with war themes, were collected posthumously by his friend, poet Siegfried Sassoon.

Anthem for Doomed Youth

What passing-bells for these who die as cattle?
    Only the monstrous anger of the guns.
    Only the stuttering rifles' rapid rattle
Can patter out their hasty orisons.
No mockeries now for them; no prayers nor bells,
    Nor any voice of mourning save the choirs, —
The shrill, demented choirs of wailing shells;
    And bugles calling for them from sad shires.

What candles may be held to speed them all?
    Not in the hands of boys, but in their eyes
Shall shine the holy glimmers of good-byes.
    The pallor of girls' brows shall be their pall;
Their flowers the tenderness of patient minds,
And each slow dusk a drawing-down of blinds.

E. E. CUMMINGS (1894–1962)

A radically modernistic challenger of conventionality in poetic usage, punctuation and thought, Cummings (who often preferred not to capitalize his name) wrote some of the most moving and innovative American verse of the twentieth century.

"anyone lived in a pretty how town"

anyone lived in a pretty how town
(with up so floating many bells down)
spring summer autumn winter
he sang his didn't he danced his did.

Women and men(both little and small)
cared for anyone not at all
they sowed their isn't they reaped their same
sun moon stars rain

children guessed(but only a few
and down they forgot as up they grew
autumn winter spring summer)
that noone loved him more by more

when by now and tree by leaf
she laughed his joy she cried his grief
bird by snow and stir by still
anyone's any was all to her

someones married their everyones
laughed their cryings and did their dance
(sleep wake hope and then)they
said their nevers they slept their dream

stars rain sun moon
(and only the snow can begin to explain
how children are apt to forget to remember
with up so floating many bells down)

one day anyone died i guess
(and noone stooped to kiss his face)
busy folk buried them side by side
little by little and was by was

all by all and deep by deep
and more by more they dream their sleep

noone and anyone earth by april
wish by spirit and if by yes.

Women and men(both dong and ding)
summer autumn winter spring
reaped their sowing and went their came
sun moon stars rain

W. H. AUDEN *(1907–1973)*

A Briton who emigrated to the United States on the eve of World War II, Auden produced a large body of first-quality verse. "Musée des Beaux Arts" was inspired by a painting by Pieter Brueghel the Elder.

Musée des Beaux Arts

About suffering they were never wrong,
The Old Masters: how well they understood
Its human position; how it takes place
While someone else is eating or opening a window or just walking
    dully along;
How, when the aged are reverently, passionately waiting
For the miraculous birth, there always must be
Children who did not specially want it to happen, skating
On a pond at the edge of the wood:
They never forgot
That even the dreadful martyrdom must run its course
Anyhow in a corner, some untidy spot
Where the dogs go on with their doggy life and the torturer's horse
Scratches its innocent behind on a tree.

In Brueghel's *Icarus*,[1] for instance: how everything turns away
Quite leisurely from the disaster; the plowman may
Have heard the splash, the forsaken cry,
But for him it was not an important failure; the sun shone
As it had to on the white legs disappearing into the green
Water; and the expensive delicate ship that must have seen
Something amazing, a boy falling out of the sky,
Had somewhere to get to and sailed calmly on.

---

[1] *Brueghel's* Icarus] "Landscape with the Fall of Icárus," a painting by Flemish artist Pieter Brueghel the Elder (c. 1525–1569) in the Musées Royaux des Beaux-Arts, Brussels.

DYLAN THOMAS *(1914–1953)*

Welsh-born Thomas led a tempestuous life, dying from alcohol abuse before his fortieth birthday. His personal turmoil bore fruit, however, in a number of the undisputed masterworks of English-language poetry, including this unforgettable villanelle.

Do Not Go Gentle into That Good Night

Do not go gentle into that good night,
Old age should burn and rave at close of day;
Rage, rage against the dying of the light.

Though wise men at their end know dark is right,
Because their words had forked no lightning they
Do not go gentle into that good night.

Good men, the last wave by, crying how bright
Their frail deeds might have danced in a green bay,
Rage, rage against the dying of the light.

Wild men who caught and sang the sun in flight,
And learn, too late, they grieved it on its way,
Do not go gentle into that good night.

Grave men, near death, who see with blinding sight
Blind eyes could blaze like meteors and be gay,
Rage, rage against the dying of the light.

And you, my father, there on the sad height,
Curse, bless, me now with your fierce tears, I pray.
Do not go gentle into that good night.
Rage, rage against the dying of the light.

Alphabetical List of Titles

Alphabetical List of First Lines

POETRY

AFRICAN-AMERICAN POETRY: An Anthology, 1773–1930, Joan R. Sherman (ed.). 96pp. 29604-0 $1.00

SELECTED POEMS, Paul Laurence Dunbar. 80pp. 29980-5 $1.00

BEST POEMS OF THE BRONTË SISTERS (ed. by Candace Ward), Emily, Anne and Charlotte Brontë. 64pp. 29529-X $1.00

GREAT POEMS BY AMERICAN WOMEN: An Anthology, Susan L. Rattiner (ed.). 224pp. (Available in U.S. only) 40164-2 $2.00

"GOD'S GRANDEUR" AND OTHER POEMS, Gerard Manley Hopkins. 80pp. 28729-7 $1.00

THE CONCORD HYMN AND OTHER POEMS, Ralph Waldo Emerson. 64pp. 29059-X $1.00

DOVER BEACH AND OTHER POEMS, Matthew Arnold. 112pp. 28037-3 $1.50

HARDY'S SELECTED POEMS, Thomas Hardy. 80pp. 28753-X $1.50

BHAGAVADGITA, Bhagavadgita. 112pp. 27782-8 $1.50

SONGS OF INNOCENCE AND SONGS OF EXPERIENCE, William Blake. 64pp. 27051-3 $1.00

BLAKE'S SELECTED POEMS, William Blake. 96pp. 28517-0 $1.00

THE CLASSIC TRADITION OF HAIKU: An Anthology, Faubion Bowers (ed.). 96pp. 29274-6 $1.50

AENEID, Vergil (Publius Vergilius Maro). 256pp. 28749-1 $2.00

SONNETS FROM THE PORTUGUESE AND OTHER POEMS, Elizabeth Barrett Browning. 64pp. 27052-1 $1.00

MY LAST DUCHESS AND OTHER POEMS, Robert Browning. 128pp. 27783-6 $1.00

POEMS AND SONGS, Robert Burns. 96pp. 26863-2 $1.00

SELECTED POEMS, George Gordon, Lord Byron. 112pp. 27784-4 $1.50

SELECTED POEMS FROM "FLOWERS OF EVIL," Charles Baudelaire. 64pp. 28450-6 $1.00

THE RIME OF THE ANCIENT MARINER AND OTHER POEMS, Samuel Taylor Coleridge. 80pp. 27266-4 $1.00

SELECTED POEMS, Emily Dickinson. 64pp. 26466-1 $1.00

SELECTED POEMS, John Donne. 96pp. 27788-7 $1.50

THE RUBÁIYÁT OF OMAR KHAYYÁM: FIRST AND FIFTH EDITIONS, Edward FitzGerald. 64pp. 26467-X $1.00

A BOY'S WILL AND NORTH OF BOSTON, Robert Frost. 112pp. (Available in U.S. only) 26866-7 $1.00

THE ROAD NOT TAKEN AND OTHER POEMS, Robert Frost. 64pp. (Available in U.S. only) 27550-7 $1.00

A SHROPSHIRE LAD, A. E. Housman. 64pp. 26468-8 $1.00

"LORD RANDAL" AND OTHER BRITISH BALLADS, Francis James Child (ed.). 64pp. 28987-7 $1.00

"TO HIS COY MISTRESS" AND OTHER POEMS, Andrew Marvell. 64pp. 29544-3 $1.00

LYRIC POEMS, John Keats. 80pp. 26871-3 $1.00

THE BOOK OF PSALMS, King James Bible. 128pp. 27541-8 $1.50

GUNGA DIN AND OTHER FAVORITE POEMS, Rudyard Kipling. 80pp. 26471-8 $1.00

THE CONGO AND OTHER POEMS, Vachel Lindsay. 96pp. 27272-9 $1.00

FAVORITE POEMS, Henry Wadsworth Longfellow. 96pp. 27273-7 $1.00

SPOON RIVER ANTHOLOGY, Edgar Lee Masters. 144pp. 27275-3 $1.50